As a mom of a hi
author addressed
read - worth you
come back to it a

— Luke H.

College application is quite intimidating, especially for us who have no experience in this. This book is perfect for understanding the process, with everything explained thoroughly. It's a relatively long reading, but definitely worth the time. With this book, we are certainly better prepared to navigate through the application process.

— W Zhang

I'm so glad I found this book at just the right time. My oldest daughter is starting her junior year of high school and the lessons I learned is this beautifully written comprehensive book are so valuable. I also recommend checking out The Ultimate College Financial Aid Guide. You don't have to figure it out alone. This book shows you the way. I highly recommend it!

— Libby Wilson

This book is very well conceptualized for parents and students about to undertake the college search and application process. It is clear, easy to read, and takes you step by step, breaking down both the concepts and the tasks. As importantly, the author regularly calms the readers, give them perspective, so they keep their anxiety in check and not get frantic about what can be a stressful process. A bonus is the well-researched list of resources with hyperlinks in the Notes. I have worked in higher education for decades and still learned much from this book! I plan to recommend it to my friends with children in high school.

— GSW

Got a high schooler who is wondering how to make it into college? My recommendation is get this book and go through it together by the end of their 10th grade year. Very comprehensive, covering everything from the application process, entrance exams, essays, financial aid, you name it. The author obviously has an insider view of the entire process.

- Dorenda Doyle

Dr. Barbu really covers all the bases. She offers a great deal of clear information taking you from the beginning to the end of the college admissions process. This is a well laid out complete guide anyone wanting to attend college will tremendously benefit from. With The Ultimate College Admissions Guide, you will save time, money, and avoid mistakes. Success is preparedness meeting opportunity. And Dr. Barbu will guide you to success though the college admissions process. A must read for anyone wanting to attend college!

- Howard Mann

I brought this book for my college bound grandkids. I love that it simplifies the process of identifying and choosing a college, applying for admissions, a, calculating costs, finding financial aid, and preparing for enrollment. The author also makes suggestions for lowering costs and improving the likelihood of admissions. So much clear and useful information is provided in this book. It streamlined the entire application process from beginning to end. This book is a must-have for anyone considering college.

- Diane Metcalf

As a parent of a high school student, I find The Ultimate College Admissions Guide essential. I don't want my student to incur on substantial debt but help her make the appropriate decisions regarding this exciting yet scary next milestone in her life. This book is a practical guide. The author provides so much information and I love that is all in one place for us to digest without getting overwhelmed or researching all over the place for answers. From college application, truth and myths, financial aid, minimizing costs and much more, this guide will help parents and students make conscious college decisions.

- Alivette Vigo

THE ULTIMATE COLLEGE ADMISSIONS GUIDE

Also By Dr. Diana Barbu

The Ultimate College Financial Aid Guide:
Understand the Aid Offer & Ask for More Money

THE ULTIMATE COLLEGE ADMISSIONS GUIDE

Help Your Teen Get In, Go Through, &
Graduate College (almost) Debt Free

Diana Barbu, PhD

Copyright © 2022 Diana Barbu, PhD

All rights reserved. No part of this publication may be reproduced, distributed, or transmitted in any form or by any means, including photocopying, recording, or other electronic or mechanical methods without the prior written permission of the publisher, except in the case of brief quotations embodied in reviews and certain other non-commercial uses permitted by copyright law.

While the author has made every effort to provide accurate Internet addresses at the time of publication, the author/publisher does not assume any responsibility for errors or changes that occur after publication.

ISBN-13: 978-1-7361875-3-1 (paper)
ISBN-13: 978-1-7361875-2-4 (e-book)

To my wonderful husband Adrian

Contents

Introduction	1
Part I COLLEGE FIT	**6**
Chapter 1: Universal Truths of College Admission	*8*
Chapter 2: College Options	*15*
Chapter 3: What Admission Officers are looking for in Future Students	*19*
Chapter 4: College Fit	*23*
Part II COLLEGE SELECTION	**30**
Chapter 5: The College Selection Funnel	*32*
Chapter 6: Building the Starter List of Colleges	*35*
Chapter 7: Balancing the List	*44*
Chapter 8: Narrowing Down the List	*77*
Chapter 9: Preparing the Essay	*102*
Part III COLLEGE APPLICATIONS	**112**
Chapter 10: College Application Plans - The Alphabet Soup ED, EA, RD, RA, PA, ...	*114*
Chapter 11: The College Application	*128*

Chapter 12: Financial Aid Applications	*142*
Part IV ADMISSION DECISIONS	**168**
Chapter 13: Types of Decisions and Next Steps	*169*
Part V MINIMIZE COLLEGE COSTS	**183**
Chapter 14: On-Time Graduation	*185*
Chapter 15: Using High School Work to Earn College Credit	*189*
Chapter 16: Using College Smarts to Graduate Almost Debt-Free	*195*
Chapter 17: The Transfer Option	*202*
Conclusion	**214**
List of Key Terms	**217**
References	**219**
Acknowledgements	**221**
About the Author	**223**
Notes	**224**

Introduction

So here we are. Your teen is ready to start the college admission process. Whether they're a junior or a senior in high school, important life decisions are coming at you fast.

You may be wondering: should my teen go to college, if so, where? How do I figure out what options are available? How do I find out which colleges have my teen's majors? How do I know which college will prepare my teen for a career of purpose that pays the bills and provides for their family? What will be their salary after graduation? How can we afford college? How do we pick the right one?

And yes, the most anxiety-producing ones: what if no college will accept them? What if all these years of hard work and extracurricular activities were all in vain?

If any of these questions swirl through your head, know that they are normal, and this book will provide you with information for each one of them. Its main goal is to help you stay sane while navigating the somewhat convoluted college admissions process.

This book will walk you through all things related to college admission. First, it will help you identify the colleges with the best fit for you and your teen. Then it will guide you through the application process, explaining how much time you need to complete it and the documents you'll need. Then we'll discuss how to keep college costs to a minimum.

Generations and generations of parents and students went through the college admission process and navigated it successfully. By the end of this book, you'll learn everything you need to know about:
- How extensive your list of options really is
- How to find colleges that offer majors that your teen is interested in
- How to make sense of various data points – graduation rates, salary after graduation, GPAs, test scores, and so on, and use them to identify the colleges with the best fit for your teen
- How to help your teen write an essay that will hook and compel admission officers
- How to make sense of the college application plans and select the ones that are best for your teen
- How much time you'll need to complete the college application, and what documents you'll need to complete it
- How to identify which financial aid applications you'll need to fill out and how to fill them out
- How to make sense of all the admission decisions and what to do if deferred or waitlisted
- How to use high school work to earn college credit and save money on the college degree

- How to help your teen pace themselves through college to avoid burn-out and graduate on time
- How to minimize college costs and graduate with a bachelor's degree almost debt-free

Here is a brief overview of how this book is structured. Part I walks you through college options and explains what they mean. Then we'll focus on the top five factors admission officers are looking for in future students. Additionally, we'll discuss the notion of fit, what it means and how to use it. More importantly, here, you'll learn the five Universal Truths associated with the college admission process. These truths will help you anchor your college admission process.

Part II walks you through your college selection. Here you'll learn how to identify colleges, build a Starter List, and use research to balance and narrow it down. Plus, you'll learn just how extensive the list of college options is, where to look for them, how to find out average high school GPAs, and whether your teen should submit their test scores. Additionally, I'll show you how to identify college costs, salaries for graduates, and the probability of finishing college in 4-years. Finally, here you'll learn about the essay and how your teen could prepare it to capture admission officers' attention. By the end of this part, you'll have your list of colleges and all the information you need to determine college fit for you and your teen.

Part III focuses on the application process. Here you'll learn about application plans and how to pick the ones that are best for your teen. This part also discusses the application documents and how much time is usually needed to prepare them. Additionally, this part explains how to prepare financial aid applications.

Part IV explains admission decisions. Here you'll learn that admission decisions are highly nuanced and may be quite complex to navigate. You'll learn the meaning of each admission decision and how to navigate it. You'll learn that the opposite of accepted is not denied.

Part V points you to existing resources to help your teen graduate college almost debt-free. Here you'll learn how to use high school work to earn college credit. Plus, you'll learn how to use college smarts to keep college costs low. Finally, this part of the book discusses the community college to university transfer option and provides strategies to help you capitalize on all the benefits associated with it.

***

While this book attempts to walk you through all the steps associated with the college admission process, feel free to use it to address your specific questions as needed. So go ahead and skip around to the sections that seem most relevant to you. For example, if you and your teen have already identified your colleges, go to chapters 7 and 8 to look up indicators that will help you research them and find the ones with the best fit.

You may already know all about the average GPAs, test scores, graduation rates, and salaries after graduation for all the colleges on your list. So if you and your teen are ready to apply but need to learn more about application plans such as Early Decision, Priority Admission, and so on, then skip to Part III.

***

All in all, I put together this book with your needs in mind. It is a comprehensive guide to help you identify the colleges with the best fit for you and your teen so that they can graduate on time and keep college costs to a minimum. Whether you start the college admission process during the sophomore, junior, or senior year of high school, this book will help you stay sane throughout this process.

Part I
COLLEGE FIT

This part demystifies the college admission process by discussing universal truths, factors that admission officers values in future students, and the main features colleges and universities.

Chapter 1 provides the five universal truths associated with the college admission process. In addition, this chapter offers perspective for this process. Here we look at college admissions from the applicant's and colleges' standpoint. Come back to this chapter whenever the process becomes too stressful and you need a bit of perspective.

Chapter 2 walks you through the main categories of colleges available in the USA. This chapter will help you understand the main features of community colleges, liberal arts colleges, and universities.

Chapter 3 presents the five most important factors that admission officers look for in future students. Here you'll learn that the weight of each one of these factors varies by college features (sector, size, and selectivity).

Finally, Chapter 4 focuses on fit. We'll discuss all the dimensions of fit and how to use them to come up with your list of colleges and decide on the best college for you and your teen.

Chapter 1: Universal Truths of College Admission

Before we begin, I would like to bring some peace of mind and share some universal truths that I learned about college admissions throughout my career.

First and foremost: you will be fine, and your teen will be fine. If you work together to develop a balanced list of colleges, you will receive more acceptances and money than you thought possible. Know that by the end of the senior year you'll have found the college with the best fit for you and your teen. So keep this in mind as we go through this process.

This is not to say that the college admission process is not stressful. As I started researching this book the amount of stress and anxiety-inducing information that I found has been staggering. The stress and anxiety are not entirely unwarranted, but the reality is that they should not keep you up at night, because there are plenty of options out there for you and your teen.

Follow along in the book, and you'll be just fine. The book shows you each facet of the college admission process so that you can understand and use it to your advantage. Knowing what to expect provides a certain level of power over the process and puts you in control.

I have been a college administrator and served in executive and senior-level positions at various colleges and universities for over a decade. Throughout this time, I came to acknowledge the value of the following universal truths. Knowing these five truths will help alleviate stress and anxiety and ensure a good night's sleep.

When the going gets tough, come back to these Universal Truths. They will provide peace of mind and help you focus on the next natural step in the college admission process.

Universal Truths
>#1: Colleges need students as much as students need colleges.
>#2: There is no formula that will guarantee college admission.
>#3: It's not about you.
>#4: You have options.
>#5: You can control the process.

Universal Truth #1: Colleges Need Students Just as much as Students Need Colleges

A 2020 survey found that 90% of senior admission officials were either concerned or **very concerned** about filling their classes and meeting their college's enrollment goals. This concern has been reported across the board for public and private colleges.[1]

Plus, only 26% of the colleges actually finished building their fall class by the May 1st deadline (the National College Decision Day). Additionally, more than half (56%) of admission directors noted that they did not fill their fall classes by July 1st, before the beginning of the fall term. In other words, many admission officials are still working on building the incoming class well after the May 1st deadline.[2]

Consequently, colleges may be willing to go the extra mile to build their classes. Until 2019 colleges were expected to honor provisions set forth by the National Association for College Admission Counseling. One of these rules asked that *"Colleges will not knowingly recruit or offer enrollment incentives to students who are already enrolled, registered, have declared their intent, or submitted contractual deposits to other institutions. May 1st is the point at which commitments to enroll become final, and colleges must respect that."*[3] However, recently, NACAC removed this provision. Now colleges can offer incentives to entice students to enroll even after they already paid the deposit and committed to a college – i.e., after May 1st.

This means that many colleges will continue to build their class after May 1st, and may offer additional incentives to students even after they have already committed to and deposited with another college.

That is not to say that you should wait and deposit with a college after May 1st. You most definitely should not push this decision after May 1st – especially as many financial aid awards may become void after this date. This is to say that you should not be surprised if you receive other enrollment offers after this date. These enrollment offers can come in the form of getting your teen an acceptance decision (getting them off the waiting or deferred list) or getting additional financial aid. For example, during the most recent admission cycles, some parents and students were surprised to receive acceptances and financial awards from colleges they did not even apply to.

This change in the NACAC rules may be invaluable information as competition for students is likely to continue to increase. So, again, do commit to a college by the May 1st deadline. Then if additional offers come in, you'll determine if they are suitable for you and your teen on a case by case basis.

Universal Truth #2: There is No Formula That Will Guarantee Admission

"There is no definite or specific combination of factors that will guarantee" admission to your desired college.[4] In other words, admission decisions are college-specific and align with the college's priorities and mission.

Each college establishes the majority of its rules and changes them as needed. The Pandemic was a great example of that. Some things that no one believed would ever change changed quickly.

Before the Pandemic, many rules remained the same year after year. For example, most of the colleges that required test scores for admission one year continued to require them again and again. The Pandemic changed that. Before the Pandemic, you could consult data aggregators to determine what has been important for a college for admission, i.e., test scores, high school GPA, class rank, number of AP or IB classes, etc. Now, college applicants need to rely more on the college websites for the most up-to-date information. So what was necessary for admission last fall may not be as crucial for admission this fall. In addition, by now, about 75% of the colleges are test-optional.[5]

In addition, turnover is also an important driver of change in admission rules. Many college presidents retired or changed jobs before or during the Pandemic. This usually brings changes to senior-level personnel. Admission officers are no exception. New presidents and personnel often revise college goals. Plus, they bring about innovation, new ideas, and new ways of helping the college achieve its goals.

Therefore, there is no guarantee that what worked in the past will work in the future. However, high school students who focus on doing their best, being continuously challenged, and seeking to better themselves will always be great candidates for admission. Therefore, colleges will continue to pay attention to them.

Universal Truth #3: It's Not About You

College acceptances maybe some of the most satisfying forms of validation one may get after years of hard work. By the same token, college rejections may feel devastating. Know that college admission decisions, especially rejections, are not about your teen. Many colleges use a holistic review to evaluate candidates for fit and pick students based on colleges' priorities.

Therefore, if your teen happens to get a rejection, know that it's not a reflection of who they are, how hard they worked, or how much they studied. One college admission officer put it best: "*Getting in, or not getting into a particular school does not change who you are, the feasibility of your goals, or define you in a substantive way … Don't let a schools decision (based on factors well outside of your control) shake your confidence … [colleges review] thousands and thousands of talented applicants that we simply don't have the capacity to admit.*" [6]

Plus, please know that one college rejecting your teen does not mean another will. So keep an open mind, build a balanced list, and acceptance letters will arrive soon.

Universal Truth #4: You Have Options

There are thousands of colleges in the US, and they all need students. Therefore, keep an open mind. As you go through this book, you'll learn about all your options and admission plans. Know that you have options. As you will learn later on in the book, you can apply to colleges as soon as August (of senior year) and, in some cases, as late as July, before the beginning of the freshman year. Be flexible. Your teen has plenty of options.

As you are getting ready to start the college admission process know that having a balanced list of colleges will help you capitalize on all the available options. Specifically, some parents and teens may be going into the college admission process with their mind set on one or two colleges they want to apply to and completely ignore the other colleges. If this is you, know that you will benefit from always having a balanced list of colleges in your back pocket, even if you never have to use it. The reality is that students never know if they'll get in, as there is no formula to guarantee admission. Plus, even if your teen gets in at this one college that they have their mind and heart set on, the financial aid packet may play a deciding role as to whether the college is an excellent financial fit.

Therefore, plan always to have a balanced list of colleges in your back pocket. It will save you from a lot of headaches later on.

Universal Truth #5: You Can Control the Process

You control the process. And this book will show you how. You can plan by learning everything you need to know about college selection, application, financial aid, and especially costs. Getting familiar with the process and planning ahead will help you mitigate the uncertainty. Once the process is less uncertain, anxiety and stress levels will decrease.

Come back to these truths when college admission questions start keeping you up at night.

Chapter 2: College Options

Before we delve deeper into college admissions let's get familiar with the existing options. This section explains the similarities and differences between public and private colleges and universities.

Post-secondary institutions can be separated into several categories depending on sector and program length.

First, the sector of an institution can be public or private. Hence, there are public institutions and private ones. To a certain extent, public institutions are funded by states; thus, costs at these institutions tend to be lower, especially for state residents.

Private institutions typically do not receive state funds. These institutions rely on students and their families, endowments, and donors for funding. Due in large part to the fact that they don't receive any state money, with very few exceptions, they tend to cost more.

Private institutions can be further classified in two categories not-for-profit and for-profit. Private not-for-profit institutions aim to provide a full educational experience and are usually geared towards providing a residential experience – students living on-campus. Private for-profit institutions are owned by large corporations that may trade on stock exchanges. Owners and stockholders expect these institutions to turn a profit. Needless to say, revenues are important for all institutions, public or private sector, but more so for private-for-profit institutions.

Second, depending on the length of their programs, institutions can be further classified into two categories: 2-year and 4-year institutions. The 2-year institutions tend to be state, junior, or community colleges. These colleges tend to offer programs that vary in length from a couple of months to a couple of years i.e., courses, certificates, apprenticeships, and associate degrees.

The 4-year institutions tend to offer baccalaureate level programs – i.e., bachelor's and above, such as masters or doctorates. These institutions are either liberal arts colleges or universities.

The following section provides information on the most common features of community colleges, liberal arts colleges, and universities.

State, Junior, or Community Colleges
- Community colleges typically offer programs that help students prepare for careers. They do this through short-term programs such as courses,

certificates*, and certifications, and longer programs, such as associate degrees.
- Some associate degrees or programs prepare students to enter the workforce immediately upon graduation (Associate of Science), while others prepare students to transfer to a university or liberal arts college (Associate of Arts).
- While most community colleges focus on programs that are 2-year or shorter, some community colleges also offer bachelor's degrees or 4-year programs. Community colleges do not offer graduate degrees (masters or above).
- **Selectivity:** An important feature of community colleges is open admission. Open admission means that community colleges accept all their applicants. In other words, community colleges are not selective.
- Usually, community colleges receive most of their funding from the state. Hence they are typically public institutions.

Universities
- Many universities offer 4-year programs – i.e., bachelor's degrees and graduate programs, masters or doctorates. The 4-year programs are commonly referred to as undergraduate programs, while the masters or doctorates are commonly referred to as graduate programs.
- Some universities may award Associate of Arts degrees to students upon request.

---

* A certificate is comprised of several college level courses; it helps students prepare for entry-level positions
(https://www.easternflorida.edu/academics/degrees-certifications/college-credit-certificate/)

- Universities tend to be larger in terms of number of students and may offer a highly diversified list of programs, such as education, nursing, engineering, music, theater, law, etc.
- **Selectivity:** The vast majority of universities are selective, i.e., they decide who gets admitted.
- Universities can be public or private (not-for-profit or for-profit).

Liberal Arts Colleges
- Liberal Arts Colleges (LAC) usually focus on undergraduate programs.[7]
- These colleges tend to be smaller in terms of the number of students and programs, compared with universities.
- Some LACs also offer a small number of graduate programs.
- **Selectivity:** The vast majority of LAC are selective.
- LACs can be public or private (not-for-profit or for-profit).

Anyone intending to pursue education after high school has lots of options, be that a certificate, associate, or bachelor's degree. This book focuses on college admissions and refers specifically to selective institutions – universities and liberal arts colleges. For simplicity, we'll call these selective institutions Colleges or Universities (C/U) or simply colleges.

Chapter 3: What Admission Officers are looking for in Future Students

So what are admission officers looking for in college applicants? While there is no formula to guarantee college admission, there are a few features that admission officers are looking for in future college students.

The National Association for College Admission Counseling (NACAC) surveys admission officers regularly. The most recent report from 2019 points to five very important features that admission officers have been looking for in future students.[8] These features are:
1. Grades in all courses
2. Grades in college preparatory courses
3. The strength of the high school curriculum
4. Admission test scores (SAT/ACT)
5. Essay or writing sample

Table and Figure 3.1 illustrate the top factors used by admission officers for decisions. While the relative importance of these factors varied slightly over time, they remained the same over the past several years. Additionally, considering that the last report was published in 2019 before most colleges switched to test-optional policies (more on testing policies in Chapter 7) it is quite possible that the top three factors became even more important for college admission decisions.

Table 3.1: Top college admission factors

	Fall 2016	Fall 2017	Fall 2018
Grades in All Courses	77%	81%	75%
Grades in College Prep Courses	77%	71%	73%
Strength of Curriculum	52%	51%	62%
Admission Test Scores (SAT, ACT)	54%	52%	46%
Essay or Writing Sample	19%	17%	23%

Source: https://www.nacacnet.org/globalassets/documents/publications/research/2018_soca/soca2019_all.pdf

Additionally, the NACAC report also found that different types of colleges emphasized some factors more than others. First, the importance of these factors varied by college sector (public or private). For example, private colleges "placed relatively more importance on the essay/writing sample, the interview, counselor and teacher recommendations, demonstrated interest, extracurricular activities, and work". On the other hand, public colleges "valued admission test scores more highly than private institutions" (p. 15).[9]

Second, college size played a role as to which factors were deemed most important. Smaller colleges "gave comparatively more weight to the interview, teacher and counselor recommendations, and demonstrated interest," while larger colleges valued test scores more (p.16).[10]

Figure 3.1: Top college admission factors

College Admission Factors

Factor	Percentage
Grades in All Courses	75%
Grades in College Prep Courses	73%
Strength of Curriculum	62%
Admission Test Scores (SAT, ACT)	46%
Essay or Writing Sample	23%

Legend: Fall 2016, Fall 2017, Fall 2018

Source: https://www.nacacnet.org/globalassets/documents/publications/research/2018_soca/soca2019_all.pdf; Figure by author.

Third, selectivity also played a role as to which factors received more consideration in the admission decision. More selective colleges emphasized "grades in college prep courses, strength of the curriculum, [...] essay/writing sample, teacher and counselor recommendations, extracurricular activities, and work" (p. 16).[11]

The report notes that admission officers work under the umbrella of college goals; they consider the "composition of the entering class as a whole to ensure that a diverse group of students with a variety of academic and extracurricular interests will enrich the campus experience."[12] In other words, remember Universal Truth #3 – *it's not about you*, it's all about the college and its priorities and goals.

Ultimately, each college examines applications in a unique way. Remember Universal Truth #2 - *there is no formula to guarantee college admission*. The best your teen can do is challenge themselves and do their best during high school. This will show progress in their studies and progression through challenging courses. Then do their best with each element of the college application. When anxiety hits, refer to Universal Truth #1 – *colleges need students just as much as students need colleges*.

Chapter 4: College Fit

Before we delve deeper into the college admission process, let's focus our attention on the notion of college fit. The reality is that college fit will inform your college selection, application, and decision processes. Therefore, having a clear understanding of how to evaluate college fit will help inform college admissions tremendously.

I have to be very honest with you and say that the notion of college fit was a mind-boggling concept for me. I understood the idea of fit as something holistic, like having a good feeling when visiting the campus or just a gut feeling about the college.

Only when I interviewed an admissions executive did I fully understand what college fit is really about. Then I wanted to find a way to communicate it so that you can use it for yourself. After thinking about it intensely, I came up with a way to make sense of this fuzzy notion.

The best way I found how to explain college fit is by building dimensions into it. Therefore, I came up with three dimensions: (1) academic, (2) personal, and (3) financial fit. These dimensions together make the college fit conversation comprehensive and meaningful. Carefully researching and evaluating these dimensions can significantly inform the entire college admission process. This discussion can help you and your teen identify the college with a great fit. In other words, identify the college with great chances of getting in and the best resources for your teen (academic fit), where your teen feels like they belong (personal fit), and can complete college debt-free or with the minimum amount of debt (financial fit).

These dimensions of fit are used extensively throughout this book. Before we go any further, let's take a moment and briefly discuss each one of these dimensions.

Academic Fit

Each college/university (C/U) has a few things, a few programs, services, and so on that it excels in. The key is to research a college thoroughly and identify these areas of excellence. The information included in the following chapters will help with that.

Academic fit can refer to (1) admission likelihood and (2) college features – offerings and services.

Admission Likelihood refers to the student's likelihood of gaining admission at the college. Let's preface this is UT#2 – *there is no formula that will guarantee college admission*. While that may be the case, we need to evaluate how your teen's statistics measure against students admitted by the college in the past. In other words, does the student have the grades, recommendations, interests, activities that will ensure that the college can help the student be successful? Therefore, how likely were students with similar features (grades, activities, etc.) to gain admission at this college? We'll delve deeper into these factors in Part II.

College Offerings refers to the college having the tools and resources to help the student succeed. For example, does the college have the programs that your teen is interested in? If so, what is the student-to-faculty ratio? Plus, does the college have support mechanisms – tutoring, advising, counseling, and so on, to help your teen succeed? We'll delve deeper into these factors in Chapter 8.

Fit occurs when a student's interest and academic credentials align with a college's areas of excellence and level of selectivity. While it may be challenging to quantify fit, it is predicated on both the student and the college having a pretty good idea about what they'd like to achieve and what they can do for each other.

Personal Fit

Personal fit refers to the level of comfort the student experiences with the college.

The college visit is one of the best ways to ascertain personal fit. Therefore, it is a good idea to visit as many colleges as possible from your list (we'll focus on how to identify your college list in Part II). Chapter 8 describes the college visit in detail.

Financial Fit

It is wise to consider financial fit before committing to a college, but not necessarily during the selection process.

Financial fit relates to the student's ability to cover education expenses. While you and your teen can ascertain academic and personal fit before applying, you'll only be able to determine financial fit once the college accepts your teen.

This is because cost information usually lags, i.e., exact costs are available for prior years rather than the upcoming year. Therefore, finding the exact cost information before applying to college can be challenging. Chapter 7 explains college costs, how to look them up, and how to find the out-of-pocket cost for your income quintile. However, you'll only be able to learn your actual out-of-pocket expenses after the college accepts your teen.

After the college acceptance letter, students receive the financial aid letter or the financial award offer. This second letter will include all the funds available to a future student if the student chooses to enroll.

Until the college provides this letter, it is best to identify costs, such as the total costs of attendance and net price, and come up with ballpark estimates. The next book in the series – The Ultimate College Financial Aid Guide: *Understand the Aid Offer & Ask For More Money.* This book will help you determine the financial fit. Scan the QR code for more details.

***

College fit is complete only when all three dimensions are considered. While it is tempting only to evaluate academic and personal fit, evaluating financial fit will help you make a smart and informed decision supporting you and your teen's futures. Because while students can take on loans and start repaying them when due, many parents also take on debt to finance their teen's college education. Therefore, the financial fit is for both the student and their parents, as it can impact both in the short and long term.

It may feel as though the college that your teen really wants to attend may not accept them or will not be affordable. While that can certainly be the case, as you are going through the college admissions process, remember that *you have options* (UT#4). One of the main goals of this book is to show you just how extensive your list of options is.

College admission is a process, and your goal, for now, is to build a diverse and balanced list of colleges. Once you have the list, I'll show you how to narrow it down and identify the college with the best fit for you and your teen.

Always keep in mind that *colleges need students as much as students need colleges* (UT#1). With that in mind, a future student who is smart and intentional about their list of colleges has very high chances of gaining admission to the majority of colleges they apply to. Then the financial aid packet will help you determine the financial fit. Finally, once the academic, personal, and financial fit are achieved, you have found your college(s).

Let me take a moment here and acknowledge that college decisions are just as irrational and constrained as any other life decision. Life is messy, and college decisions are no exception. As you are at the beginning of this process, my goal is to help you explore all your options and then provide you with a way to evaluate every one of them to help you make the best decision possible. You may not use each indicator discussed in this book, but at least you know it exists, and you know how to make sense of it, if it is relevant to you, and that you could use it if needed. Hence, this book aims to provide you with more information to determine fit than a college's free ice cream machines, beautiful campus, or concierge services.

Summary

Overall the purpose of this part has been to help you get familiar with the available options – community colleges, liberal arts colleges, and universities. Then help you understand their most common features so that you can use this information to inform college selection and application.

Then, as you are entering the college selection process, I wanted you to get a clear idea about the factors that admission officers focus on in future students and that the weight of these factors varies by college characteristics.

Moreover, we discussed the concept of college fit. We'll come back to it repeatedly, as the vast majority of this book aims to help you understand it and use it for your benefit.

Finally, the following five Universal Truths of college admission are important:

UT#1: Colleges need students as much as students need colleges.
UT#2: There is no formula that will guarantee college admission.
UT#3: It's not about you.
UT#4: You have options.
UT#5: You can control the process.

Keep them in mind while reading and working through the following parts and chapters. These truths can anchor your college admission process and give you a safe place to come back to when the college process becomes overwhelming and when stress keeps you up at night.

Part II
COLLEGE SELECTION

This part helps you understand how extensive your list of college options is. This part will help you identify a Starter List of colleges. In these chapters, you will learn how to thoroughly research colleges and find the ones with the best fit.

Here is where we lay down the foundation and start building on it. This part is essential in the college admission process as it can help you learn how college selection can get your teen closer to college graduation. In this part, you'll learn how to identify the college that will increase your teen's probability of graduating college on time and with the least amount of debt.

The reality is that your teen doing their best during high school is good, but not paying attention to the indicators discussed in this part may impact their future.

This part will help you determine your teen's probability of graduating college in 4 years with the least amount of debt. Here you'll learn how much debt is too much, should you need to take on debt to finance your college education. Finally, you'll learn everything you need to know about what to look for to ascertain academic and personal fit with a college.

Chapter 5: The College Selection Funnel

Now that we have a clear idea about the factors admission officers focus on, let's find out what college options are available.

There are many ways to select colleges. For example, some people may suggest examining colleges' core values, while others tell you to focus on their commitment to the environment, diversity, and other current issues. Yet, others will recommend focusing on the salary or earnings once a student completes the degree, the internship opportunities, the network of college alumni, and so on.

While all of this is sound advice, the following model encourages you to go deeper and add a little bit of data and science to the college selection process. Before you panic, know that the process is really not that complicated. Learning a college's stats can significantly inform the selection and help parents and students identify the colleges with a great academic, personal, and financial fit.

Let's face it; the sooner students graduate from college, the sooner they'll be able to compete for a full-time position and secure a good salary. Of course, that is not to say that students should rush through college, but research shows that staying in college past the 4- or 5-year mark can be quite costly.

This college selection model shows you how to identify and select colleges to maximize the probability of completing a college degree in 4-years debt-free or with a minimal amount of debt.

The following college selection model involves a funnel. We start at the top of the funnel with a few factors to identify a large number of colleges. These colleges will form the Starter List. Next, we'll focus on researching these colleges to balance and then narrow down the list. This book will guide you every step of the way.

Figure 5.1: The college selection funnel

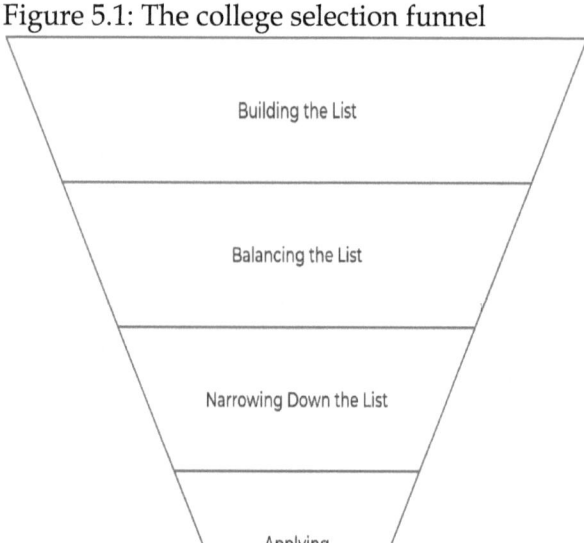

Chapter 6: Building the Starter List of Colleges

The first step is putting together the Starter List of colleges. We will have identified about 25 to 40 colleges for further research by the end of this chapter.

But first, let's discuss one of the most important data sources that we'll use throughout the book. The first source is College Navigator.

College Navigator is one of the most comprehensive data aggregators currently available. It is maintained by the federal government and sits on a database that collects data from colleges and universities across the country. Each college and university that receives money from the federal government must report data back to this database annually.

This is a great source of information because it provides the most up-to-date statistics available for most colleges.

College Navigator captures data related to enrollment, admissions, costs, financial aid, etc. Figure 6.1 includes all the areas for which you can get data. As we progress through the book, we'll explore more of these areas in detail and use this information to refine the list of colleges and determine academic fit.

Figure 6.1: College Navigator sections

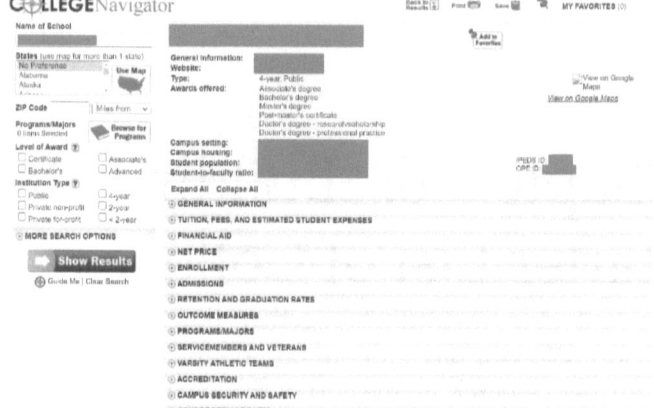

Source: College Navigator https://nces.ed.gov/collegenavigator/

We will be using College Navigator extensively as we go forward. Here are a few things to keep in mind about the data. First, the data are always lagging. In other words, colleges and universities report data for the previous year. By the time the aggregators make the data available, the data may be a little more than one-year old.

***

All in all, I am partial to College Navigator because it includes the most recent data available for all colleges. Plus, all the data follow the same specifications, and I know how much effort goes into preparing, checking, and cross-checking the data. Besides colleges running checks on their data, the federal government also performs important checks to ensure data accuracy and validity.

As you progress through this section, you may want to open College Navigator (https://nces.ed.gov/collegenavigator/) in a browser and follow along.

College Navigator has a neat feature that helps students and parents build college lists. I am using this feature to put together my sample Starter List.

The following section presents a few factors you may want to consider for building your Starter List of colleges. To illustrate the points discussed in each section I am building my Starter List of colleges and including them in a table at the end of each chapter.

Location or Distance from Home

Some of the first conversations about college revolve around "where" to go to college. A recent survey showed that about 50% of parents wanted their teens to attend college within a 250-mile radius from home. More than 60% of teens wanted to attend college further away.[13] I have to confess that I was like most students, and my mom was like most parents. But, ultimately, I went to college in my hometown, and it was a great experience.

Location can be qualified as the state or the distance in miles from a zip code.

Majors or Programs of Study

Go to College Navigator and click on "Browse for Programs," and select all the programs of interest. If your teen has not yet decided, they may choose all the programs that appeal to them.

By selecting majors now, your teen would be able to narrow down the number of Colleges/Universities (C/U) that end up on the Starter List. It should also be noted that colleges establish and sunset majors regularly. So if your teen is keenly interested in a specific college but cannot find their desired major, it is a good idea to contact the admission office and inquire if the college has any plans to offer the desired major in the future.

Plus, selecting majors now may help later on when your teen may want to change majors. Statistically, about 33% of students change majors at least once while in college.[14] Changing majors within the same C/U tends to be way easier than transferring to another one that offers the desired major.

It's Okay to be Undecided
It is quite common for students to be undecided or not know what they'd like to major in when thinking of college. One goal of college is to help students identify what they'd like to study and eventually pursue as a career. The freshman year exposes students to different classes and presents them with plenty of opportunities to choose a major. Plus, colleges have various mechanisms that can help students select a major. On the one hand, academic advisers can help with this decision. On the other hand, many colleges have very well-staffed career centers. These advisers can help students identify the best majors for their goals.

Going to college undecided is not as uncommon as you may think. In fact, 20-50% of students go to college undecided.[15] Even students who go to college decided on a major may change it at least once throughout their studies.[16]

Also, remember this is just the first step. For now, we want to identify a Starter List of colleges to see what options are available. Once we finalize this list, we'll research colleges further.

College Size & Campus Setting
Another factor commonly used in identifying colleges is the size of the student body. Some people love small groups, where everyone knows everyone else, and there is a strong sense of community. Others, however, may like the anonymity and the ability to interact with new individuals often. There is no right or wrong approach, whichever may be the case for you. Therefore, feel free to decide on an approximate number and use that value. Go to College Navigator and select "More Search Options," and enter information on the size of the student body (referred to as: "Undergraduate Student Enrollment").

Other Characteristics
Take a quick look at the remaining options and select the ones that seem appropriate for you and your teen. For example, I suggest that from the "Level of Award" check Bachelor and Advanced, and from "Institution Type" select 4-year.

If your teen is interested in playing varsity sports or attending athletic events, you can select the sport(s) in the "Varsity Athletic Teams" section. Once comfortable with the options selected, click on "Show Results."

***

Depending on how many criteria you specified, your list can include anywhere from a few to a few dozen colleges. The overall goal in the Starter List is to provide you with exposure to those Colleges/Universities (C/U) that meet your specifications.

You may repeat this step as many times as needed. Feel free to fine-tune each indicator and identify additional colleges you may want to research further.

Ta-da! Now you have the Starter List. Coming up with the Starter List is one of the most important first steps to the college admissions process.

Once you are satisfied with the colleges on your list, click on "Export Results." This way, you can download your list into an Excel file. I recommend this step since we'll be adding additional information and indicators to that file as we go through the chapters of this book. You can also "Save" the list and access it later.

For illustration purposes, I searched for colleges using various criteria and ended up with a list of 30 colleges in my Starter List (Table 6.1). The Starter List includes information such as the address, college type, campus housing, student population, types of awards offered, graduation rate, net price, and so on.

The DSSL Excel File

For ease of use, I put together an excel file with all the columns and information that we'll use to get a comprehensive idea of academic fit. I called this file: Diana's Sample Starter List (DSSL).

The DSSL file includes all the columns provided by the College Navigator through the "Export Results" option, plus all the additional columns that we'll add in the following chapters. Specifically, you will get a file with about 16 columns through the College Navigator "Export." Then you'll have to add about 12 more to it.

The DSSL file includes all these 28 columns plus three colleges as a sample. Scan the QR code below to download the DSSL file. You can copy and paste all the 12 column headings from the DSSL file and add them to your Starter List that you'll download from College Navigator.

Alternatively, you can add the columns as you progress through this book.

***

In the next chapter, we'll balance the list by adding information to it and combining it with your teen's academic achievement information.

Table 6.1: The Starter List of colleges

Name	Address	Website	Type	Campus setting	Campus housing	Student population	Undergraduate students	Graduation Rate	Transfer-Out Rate	Cohort Year	Net Price
College 1	Address	Website	4-year, Public	City: Midsize	Yes	9,626	7,818	53%	24%	Fall 2013	$14,610
College 2	Address	Website	4-year, Public	City: Midsize	Yes	42,450	33,270	83%	5%	Fall 2013	$12,568
College 3	Address	Website	4-year, Private not-for-profit	Town: Distant	Yes	1,528	947	47%	NA	Fall 2013	$23,103
College 4	Address	Website	4-year, Public	City: Small	Yes	11,270	8,590	40%	41%	Fall 2013	$13,502
College 5	Address	Website	4-year, Public	City: Small	Yes	6,122	5,778	23%	47%	Fall 2013	$12,500
College 6	Address	Website	4-year, Public	Town: Distant	Yes	2,950	2,498	38%	40%	Fall 2013	$10,904
College 7	Address	Website	4-year, Public	City: Midsize	Yes	52,407	35,405	88%	3%	Fall 2013	$10,457
College 8	Address	Website	4-year, Public	Town: Remote	Yes	16,436	12,995	47%	8%	Fall 2013	$12,951
College 9	Address	Website	4-year, Public	City: Midsize	Yes	7,877	6,501	38%	36%	Fall 2013	$11,361
College 10	Address	Website	4-year, Public	Town: Fringe	Yes	2,624	2,293	35%	42%	Fall 2013	$13,075
College 11	Address	Website	4-year, Private not-for-profit	City: Large	Yes	4,164	2,928	52%	8%	Fall 2013	$24,020
College 12	Address	Website	4-year, Private not-for-profit	Town: Distant	Yes	2,876	2,394	52%	NA	Fall 2013	$33,420
College 13	Address	Website	4-year, Public	City: Large	Yes	17,117	14,734	67%	10%	Fall 2013	$9,857
College 14	Address	Website	4-year, Public	City: Small	Yes	30,460	24,594	79%	13%	Fall 2013	$23,562
College 15	Address	Website	4-year, Public	City: Midsize	Yes	8,066	7,787	23%	50%	Fall 2013	$9,781
College 16	Address	Website	4-year, Private not-for-profit	City: Midsize	Yes	8,740	4,865	66%	28%	Fall 2013	$21,696
College 17	Address	Website	4-year, Private not-for-profit	City: Midsize	Yes	797	754	50%	NA	Fall 2013	$13,254
College 18	Address	Website	4-year, Private not-for-profit	City: Midsize	No	833	365	33%	33%	Fall 2013	$3,905
College 19	Address	Website	4-year, Public	City: Midsize	Yes	5,188	4,523	34%	33%	Fall 2013	$14,559
College 20	Address	Website	4-year, Public	City: Small	Yes	12,557	9,521	46%	9%	Fall 2013	$7,515
College 21	Address	Website	4-year, Private not-for-profit	Town: Distant	Yes	2,389	2,340	28%	NA	Fall 2013	$17,185
College 22	Address	Website	4-year, Private not-for-profit	Suburb: Small	Yes	2,902	2,889	53%	NA	Fall 2013	$23,751
College 23	Address	Website	4-year, Private not-for-profit	City: Midsize	Yes	1,008	1,008	49%	NA	Fall 2013	$21,738
College 24	Address	Website	4-year, Private not-for-profit	City: Midsize	Yes	3,036	2,192	33%	44%	Fall 2013	$19,990

Name	Address	Website	Type	Campus setting	Campus housing	Student population	Undergraduate students	Graduation Rate	Transfer-Out Rate	Cohort Year	Net Price
College 25	Address	Website	4-year, Private not-for-profit	Suburb: Midsize	Yes	416	416	68%	5%	Fall 2013	$45,346
College 26	Address	Website	4-year, Public	City: Midsize	Yes	4,190	3,750	33%	36%	Fall 2013	$13,476
College 27	Address	Website	4-year, Private not-for-profit	Town: Distant	Yes	995	872	41%	46%	Fall 2013	$20,612
College 28	Address	Website	4-year, Private not-for-profit	Suburb: Small	Yes	10,912	7,843	49%	36%	Fall 2013	$19,843
College 29	Address	Website	4-year, Public	Town: Distant	Yes	7,031	5,844	64%	31%	Fall 2013	$20,823
College 30	Address	Website	4-year, Public	City: Large	Yes	44,246	32,684	75%	11%	Fall 2013	$9,787

Chapter 7: Balancing the List

Now that we have the Starter List, we will add information to it. This information will help us understand where we stand in relation to students who were accepted and enrolled in the past. Once all the information is in one place, we'll be able to identify the colleges with a high likelihood of getting accepted and a good academic fit.

The following sections discuss high school GPA, tests scores, and costs.

The High School GPA

As you probably remember from Chapter 3, one of the most important factors identified by admission officers for college admission decisions was "grades in all [high school] courses," in essence the HSGPA (p. 2)[17].
Plus, a 2007 study published by UC Berkeley using unweighted HSGPA found that "high-school grade point average (HSGPA) is consistently the best predictor" of college freshman grades, cumulative college GPA, and college graduation (p. 1).[18]

Therefore, the first indicator we'll add to the Starter List is the average High School GPA (HSGPA). This is the average HSGPA value for the students who enrolled in the college in the past. However, before we go forward, let's discuss terminology.

Students – Applied, Admitted, Enrolled

Throughout this book, we'll refer to three main categories of students:
- Applicants – students who applied for admission
- Admits – students who were admitted out of the ones that applied
- Enrolled – students who paid the deposit and attended a specific college (after being admitted). Enrolled, therefore, excludes students who were admitted but chose to enroll in a different college.

GPA - Weighted vs. Un-weighted

Let's take a moment to clarify the distinction between unweighted and weighted GPA. The HSGPA is calculated by converting letter grades to points or numbers. According to the Common Data Set, "the most common system of assigning numbers to grades" is as follows: "four points for an A, three points for a B, two points for a C, one point for a D, and no points for an E or F."[19] That being said, the difference between weighted and unweighted GPA lies in course difficulty.

Unweighted HSGPA

The Unweighted GPA refers to the average high school GPA where the course difficulty is not considered. For the unweighted GPA calculations, for every A a student got during high school, they will receive 4 points; for every B, they will receive 3 points, and so on. For example, let's consider Student 1, who completed only two courses during high school – AP Calculus and Physical Education. Let's assume that Student 1 got an A in both courses. As a grade of A corresponds to 4 points, their unweighted HSGPA is (4.0 + 4.0) / 2 = 4.0. Let's take another example, Student 2 completed ten (10) courses during high school and received A's in nine of them and B in one of them. Their unweighted average high school GPA (HSGPA) will be (9 x 4.0 + 1 x 3.0) / 10 = 3.9.

Weighted HSGPA

Weighted HSGPA calculations are a bit different. This GPA considers the difficulty of high school courses when assigning points to letter grades. When course difficulty is considered, a grade of A receives 5 points, a grade of B receives 4 points, and so on. So now, let's go back to Student 1, who completed only two courses during high school - AP Calculus and Physical Education. Let's assume that Student 1 got an A in both courses. As one of the courses is an AP course (i.e., more challenging), the A grade corresponds to 5 points, so the weighted HSGPA for Student 1 is (5.0 + 4.0) / 2 = 4.5.

Now, let's focus on Student 2. Let's say that 7 of the ten courses were AP courses, and the rest were regular high school courses. Now let's assume that the student received a grade of A in all seven AP courses, a grade of A in two other high school courses, and a grade of B in a regular high school course. Now the weighted average

HSGPA for Student 2 is (7 x 5.0 + 2 x 4.0 + 1 x 3.0) / 10 = 4.6.

As you can see, the weighted and unweighted average HSGPA differ significantly for the two students in our examples. The GPAs are likely to increase if students complete more challenging courses, secure good grades in them, and colleges use the weighted GPA calculations.

***

Now, if only things were this easy. In an article published in *Washington Post* in 2018, Jeffrey Selingo noted that in terms of admission decisions, the way the HSGPA is calculated, and high school transcripts are used might vary by college and change over time. For example, he noted that "colleges are not consistent in how they assess high school grades in admission decisions." [20] Some colleges may use the unweighted HSGPA to decide. Others, on the other hand, may look at the transcript and decide which courses carry more weight for admission and may re-calculate (weigh) the GPA accordingly. [21]

Selingo noted that the key for a successful college application was for students to challenge themselves in high school and demonstrate growth over time. [22]

***

Now let's go to the Excel file with our Starter List of colleges and add the following two columns:
- "Average High School GPA (HSGPA)"
- "Average HSGPA Determination"

Next we'll focus on how to fill out these columns.

Adding the "Average HSGPA" to the Starter List

The federal government does not collect the HSGPA data. Therefore, College Navigator does not provide any information on this. Here are a few ways to get information about the average HSGPA:
1. the college website,
2. the Common Data Set (CDS), or
3. data reported to other organizations through the CDS.

The College Website

One way to find the average HSGPA data is by researching a college's website. Many colleges provide the average HSGPA for their prior class on their websites. You may also be able to find guidance on what the college is looking for in terms of student achievement, courses required for admission, and other elements that would make an application stand out.

Make sure you check the admission websites for the colleges in your list and add the average HSGPA information to your Starter List. You may also want to set up a document to keep track of specific requirements for each college. Finally, some colleges specify the HSGPA they would consider for future students in this section.

The Common Data Set

Another way to access the average HSGPA information is to check out the values reported by colleges through the Common Data Set (CDS).

The CDS is another very important data source we'll use throughout this book. The CDS data will help with determining certain aspects of academic fit.

The CDS is a joint project of the College Board, Princeton Review and US News & World Report. These three ranking agencies collaborated to create a form for colleges to use in submitting data to them. The group may review and revise the document annually. Other external organizations and college media groups use this information to produce reports that compare colleges using standardized measures.

One of the main features of the CDS is that it may include the HSGPA if colleges choose to report it. It is important to know that:
- Colleges are not required to complete the CDS. Hence some colleges do not complete it or don't complete it every year.
- Colleges are not required to complete each section.
- The data reported through CDS are usually used for rankings and get centralized and published by various data aggregators.

The CDS captures data points that are different form the ones captured by the federal government. Therefore, in a way, the CDS complements the data captured by College Navigator. It includes information on HSGPA, waitlists, admission requirements for regular and transfer students, and so on.

The CDS is separated into different sections. In this chapter, we'll focus on section C of the CDS. Section C includes freshman admissions data, including the average HSGPA, test scores, and admission requirements.

The average HSGPA is included in element C12. Plus, element C11 includes the percentage of students reporting HSGPA in different ranges. Here are a few things to keep in mind regarding the average HSGPA:
- It appears that the CDS asks colleges to report the un-weighted HSGPA.
- Some colleges provide both the weighted and un-weighted HSGPA.
- Some colleges leave these sections empty.
- If you cannot find HSGPA ranges in the most recent CDS, try looking at an earlier one.

Again, remember that:
- Colleges are not required to complete the CDS.
- Colleges are not required to complete each section or element.
- Colleges are not required to post the CDS on their websites.

The best way to find the CDS is by googling the name of the college and CDS. Usually, the CDS will be listed under the Institutional Research section of the website.

Other Sources

Another way to access the average HSGPA information is to check out data reported to external organizations, such as the Princeton Review, College Board, or others.

Some of these aggregators publish the CDS data and the average HSGPA for a past incoming class.

Use these resources to find the average HSGPA for a prior incoming class for as many colleges as possible. Then add the HSGPAs for your colleges to your Starter List.

Adding the "Average HSGPA Determination" to the Starter List

Now that you added all the average HSGPA that you could find to the colleges in your Starter List let's use these values to determine the likelihood of acceptance. Again, these determinations are estimates intended to give future students an idea of where their GPA stands in relation to students from a prior incoming class.

Now we'll go through the Starter List and make the determinations using the average HSGPA values. If your HSGPA is:
- higher than the average, assign "Safety" to the college
- about the same as the average, assign "Reach" to the college
- lower than the average, assign "Dream" to the college

Table 7.1 provides my HSGPA determinations, using a HSGPA of 3.78. Unfortunately, I couldn't find the average HSGPA for several colleges on my list. So here's what my Starter List looks like now that I added these two values.

It bears repeating that there is no hard and fast rule regarding admission decisions. For example, a certain HSGPA or test score will not guarantee admission. It is also possible that someone with a GPA higher than the average HSGPA may get rejected, while someone with a lower GPA may get accepted.

Remember Universal Truth #3 – *it's not about you(r) teen*, as admission decisions are college-specific and align with the college's priorities and mission.

Table 7.1: Starter List with average HSGPA and determination

Name	Campus housing	Avg. HSGPA	Avg. HSGPA Determination
College 1	Yes	3.47	Safety
College 2	Yes	4.07	Dream
College 3	Yes	not found	
College 4	Yes	3.07	Safety
College 5	Yes	not found	
College 6	Yes	3.27	Safety
College 7	Yes	4.5	Dream
College 8	Yes	3.37	Safety
College 9	Yes	2.96	Safety
College 10	Yes	3.29	Safety
College 11	Yes	3.53	Safety
College 12	Yes	3.24	Safety
College 13	Yes	3.91	Reach
College 14	Yes	3.9	Reach
College 15	Yes	3.27	Safety
College 16	Yes	3.86	Reach
College 17	Yes	not found	
College 19	Yes	3.39	Safety
College 20	Yes	3.58	Safety
College 21	Yes	3.22	Safety
College 22	Yes	3.49	Safety
College 23	Yes	3.43	Safety
College 24	Yes	3.26	Safety
College 25	Yes	2.8	Safety
College 26	Yes	not found	
College 27	Yes	not found	
College 28	Yes	3.13	Safety
College 29	Yes	3.47	Safety
College 30	Yes	3.98	Dream

Standardized Tests

The second set of values that we will add to the Starter List is the standardized test scores. Many colleges have dropped the standardized testing requirement for students applying for the Fall of 2021. However, at the beginning of 2021, some colleges and states announced they would require standardized test scores for the Fall 2022 admission cycle.

The use of standardized test scores for admission has been controversial. I won't get into the merits of using or not using test scores for admission. However, what we do know is that there is significant uncertainty around test scores, and this uncertainty is likely to continue.

So far, colleges have been employing one of three test-score models for college admission:
  (1) required – colleges require that students submit test scores to be considered for admission;
  (2) optional - colleges do not require test scores but may consider them if students decide to submit them; or
  (3) blind - colleges do not allow students to submit test scores.

At this point, the University of California is test blind.[23] More than 1,700 colleges (73%) of the colleges are test-optional for 2022.[24] All in all, colleges usually decide which testing model to follow.

While many colleges went test-optional during the 2021 and 2022 admission cycles, many students signed up to take the test. Sometimes they flew or drove several hours to other states to do it. Therefore, even though colleges were test-optional, many students still submitted test scores to be considered for admission.

Now that you have a clear understanding of the models that colleges use for admission consideration, let's add the following columns to the C/Us included in the Starter List:

- "Testing Model" - Required, Optional, or Blind
- "SAT/ACT 25th-75th Percentile"
- "Standardized Testing Determination"

This information will be handy, especially if your teen plans to or has already taken the SAT/ACT.

Adding "Testing Model" Information to the Starter List

To identify the test model used by the colleges in your list, go to the college's website. Typically, you should be able to find it in the Admissions section.

To fill out the first column, "Testing Model," I researched each college's website to determine its testing policy. Several colleges in my Starter List required test scores, some were test-optional, and a few were test blind.

Adding the "SAT/ACT 25th - 75th Percentile" Test Scores

Now let's add historical test scores to the Starter List. Here are two ways to get to these values – the College Navigator and the Common Data Set.

College Navigator. These data are reported to the federal government (College Navigator) annually in quartiles.

Therefore, we can access the test score values for the 25th and 75th percentiles. These values show that 50% of the students who enrolled in a particular college scored between the 25th and 75th percentile, while the remaining 50% scored above and below these percentiles. For example, if the SAT scores listed in College Navigator for College A are 900 and 1,100 then 25% of the students scored at or below 900, 50% scored between 900 and 1,100, and 25% scored above 1,100.

These scores are only for those students who enrolled in a particular C/U. Remember, enrolled students are the students who applied, were admitted, and attended a specific college.

So here's how you can look up the test scores for the colleges in your list and add these scores to the "SAT/ACT 25th-75th Percentile" column:

- Go to College Navigator https://nces.ed.gov/collegenavigator and search for your college
- Scroll down and click on the "Admissions" section
- Get the 25th and 75th percentile values for SAT/ACT and add them to your Starter List
- Repeat these steps for every college in your Starter List.

Figure 7.1: The Admissions section in College Navigator

⊖ ADMISSIONS

Undergraduate application fee (2020-2021)			$30
UNDERGRADUATE ADMISSIONS FALL 2020			
	TOTAL	MALE	FEMALE
Number of applicants	63,691	24,757	38,934
Percent admitted	32%	33%	32%
Percent admitted who enrolled	29%	29%	29%
ADMISSIONS CONSIDERATIONS	REQUIRED	RECOMMENDED	CONSIDERED BUT NOT REQUIRED
Secondary school GPA	X		
Secondary school rank			X
Secondary school record	X		
Completion of college-preparatory program	X		
Admission test scores (SAT/ACT)	X		
TOEFL (Test of English as a Foreign language)	X		

TEST SCORES: FALL 2020 (ENROLLED FIRST-TIME STUDENTS)

STUDENTS SUBMITTING SCORES	NUMBER	PERCENT
SAT	3,916	65%
ACT	2,093	35%

TEST SCORES	25TH PERCENTILE*	75TH PERCENTILE**
SAT Evidence-Based Reading and Writing	620	680
SAT Math	600	670
ACT Composite	27	31
ACT English	26	33
ACT Math	25	29

NOTES:
* 25% of students scored at or below
** 25% of students scored above

It is important to note that only colleges that require test scores for admission must report them to the federal government. Some test-optional colleges, however, may report scores as well. So, all in all, you may be able to find test scores for many colleges on your list, even if they were not required to report them.

The "Admissions" section in College Navigator includes lots of data, such as the application fee, the number of applicants, the percent of admitted applicants, and the percent of admitted students who enrolled. Here you can also find the percent of students who submitted SAT or ACT scores and the 25th and 75th percentile scores for each section of the SAT and ACT. I like the 25th and 75th percentiles values because they provide better information than averages.

***

The Common Dataset (CDS) is the other data source when it comes to test scores. It provides average test scores and sometimes ranges for these scores. This information is typically provided in element C9 of Section C.

Section C also has valuable information regarding admission requirements for the most recent incoming class. Here you'll be able to find how important test scores, HSGPA, class rank, interview, extracurricular activities, essay, and so on were for the admission decision.

You'll also find the high school academic units required or recommended for future students. This information can help you identify if the college has specific requirements regarding Math, English, Science, etc. This section may be significant for planning courses for the junior and senior years in high school.

While the CDS can provide valuable information, some colleges may not report this data.

Adding the "Standardized Testing Determination"

Using the data from the "SAT/ACT 25th-75th Percentile" column, we'll go through the Starter List of colleges and fill out the "Standardized Testing Determination" column.

Depending on your scores, we'll assign one of the following values – Safety, Reach, or Dream. If your standardized score is:
- about the same or higher than the 75th percentile score, we'll assign "Safety" to the college
- somewhere between the 25th and 75th percentile, we'll assign "Reach" to the college
- lower than the 25th percentile score, we'll assign "Dream" to the college

Here are some benefits of adding test scores to the Starter List. First, this information will help you decide on whether you'd like to apply to the college. Second, these scores will help you determine whether to submit the scores as part of the application for test-optional schools. I would consider submitting my scores to test-optional schools if my score is close to or above the 75th percentile value.

Again, back to Universal Truth #2 - *there are no guarantees for college admission*. Many people may tell you that their test scores were below the 25th percentile, and they got accepted and maybe even got some scholarships. And that might be true. Each college uses a unique admission formula, which can change over time as colleges' priorities shift. Plus, test scores are only one part of the admission application.

It might be tempting to think that the 75th percentile values are similar for many colleges. So I plotted the 75th percentile values for SAT for all the colleges that admitted more than 1% of their applicants and reported the scores – see Figure 7.2. The test score values are for the students who enrolled in college in Fall 2019.

Here are a few things to keep in mind with the SAT scores: (1) the 75th percentile scores varied widely across all selective C/Us, and (2) only 25% of these institutions had the 75th percentile score above 1,300.

That is to say that it's not about the percentile that your teen secured through testing that matters for admission. Instead, it is about how your teen's score compares to the scores of the students who enrolled at the same college in the past.

***

Also, as you look up test scores to add to your Starter List, you may not find them for some test-optional colleges, as they do not have to report them. Therefore, I downloaded all the test scores for Fall 2019, the last year when the pandemic did not impact college admission. These data may be helpful to anchor your teen scores so that you both can decide whether to send them in.

Figure 7.2: SAT Evidence-Based Reading and Writing & Math 75th percentile scores - Fall 2019

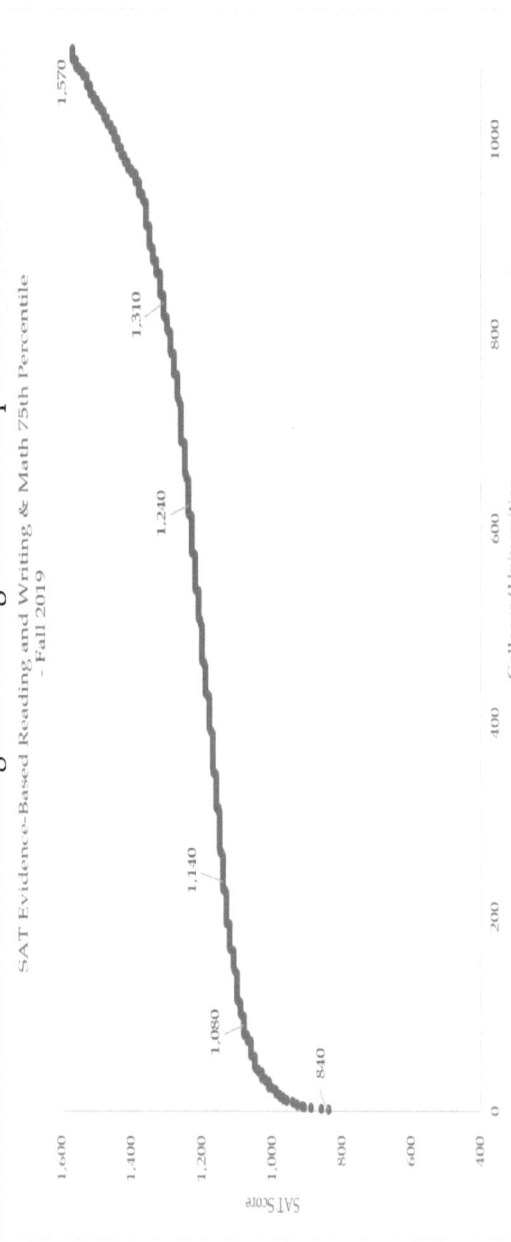

Source: IPEDS

Another reason for making these values available is that a test-optional policy may lead to higher scores. Specifically, it may be that only the students who scored higher submit their scores for admission. If that happens, the 25th to 75th percentiles may go up significantly, while the number of students who submitted scores may decrease. This may happen especially starting with the Fall 2021 admission cycle. This may make it challenging for students to assess how they compare with the 75th percentile and whether to submit their scores.

However, historical data indicates that the 25th and 75th percentile values have remained relatively stable over time. For example, a 2021 survey of admission officers found that 74% of the respondents did not expect their institution to "admit students it probably would not have admitted in prior years" (p. 11).[25] Therefore, even if the 25th - 75th percentiles move higher for test-optional colleges, the Fall 2019 scores may be a helpful baseline to determine how your teen's 75th percentile scores compare with the historical data points.

The source for the Fall 2019 data is the same – the National Center for Educational Statistics - the same database that supports College Navigator. These values are also freely available, but looking for them is more involved. Scan the QR code included below to download the Fall 2019 scores.

***

Before we go forward, let's discuss open admission colleges. Open admission colleges are the colleges that take in everyone who applies. Therefore, they do not pick and choose their students. These are typically junior, state or community colleges. Plus, some other colleges and universities may be open admission, also. If you find the following language in the Admissions section: "This institution has an open admission policy. Contact the institution for more information." The C/U is open access – i.e., admits/accepts everyone.

Students interested in attending an Open Admission college only need to apply and then get ready to register for and attend classes. Also, another important feature of Open Admission institutions is that they accept applications all the time. Therefore, there is no deadline for applying.

***

Here's what my Starter List looks like with the standardized testing information. First, I added the three columns ("Testing Model," "SAT/ACT 25th-75th Percentile," and "Standardized Testing Determination").

Then, I followed the steps and added values for these columns for each college in my Starter List.

Table 2 shows my determination for the 3rd column with an SAT score of 1,150. Also, there are a few test-optional colleges on my list where my SAT score of 1,150 is close to or higher than the 75th percentile score. If I decide to apply to these colleges, I'll submit my SAT scores for admission.

Due to space consideration, many columns from the Starter List are not displayed in table 7.2. In other words, try not to separate these columns from your Starter List, as the goal is to have all the information on one page so that you can look at all the data points simultaneously.

Table 7.2: The Starter List with standardized test scores and determinations

Name	Avg. HSGPA	Avg. HSGPA Determination	Testing Policy	SAT 25th-75th Percentile	Standardized Testing Determination
College 1	3.47	Safety	Required	1,030 - 1,160	Safety
College 2	4.07	Dream	Optional	1,200 - 1,340	Dream
College 3	not found		Optional	670 - 900	Safety
College 4	3.07	Safety	Blind		
College 5	not found		Optional	668 - 890	Safety
College 6	3.27	Safety	Required	940 - 1,120	Safety
College 7	4.5	Dream	Blind		
College 8	3.37	Safety	Required	930 - 1,090	Safety
College 9	2.96	Safety	Required	860 - 1,100	Safety
College 10	3.29	Safety	Optional	850 - 960	Safety
College 11	3.53	Safety	Blind		
College 12	3.24	Safety	Blind		
College 13	3.91	Reach	Optional	1,090 - 1,260	Reach
College 14	3.9	Reach	Required	1,150 - 1,320	Reach
College 15	3.27	Safety	Blind		
College 16	3.86	Reach	Blind		
College 17	not found		Required	940 - 1,120	Safety
College 18	3.39	Safety	Open Admission		
College 19	3.58	Safety	Blind		
College 20	3.22	Safety	Blind		
College 21	3.49	Safety	Optional	880 - 1,110	Safety
College 22	3.43	Safety	Blind		
College 23	3.26	Safety	Blind		
College 24	2.8	Safety	Required	1,000 - 1,160	Safety
College 25	not found		Blind		
College 26	not found		Optional	880-1,020	Safety
College 27	3.13	Safety	Optional	1,000-1,148	Safety
College 28	3.47	Safety	Blind		
College 29	3.98	Dream	Optional	1,110 - 1,260	Safety
College 30	not found		Blind		

College Costs

College can be expensive! Therefore, being smart about college selection and the overall admission process can help your teen keep college costs low.

This book aims to help you find the college with the best fit for you and your teen. This section discusses college costs, sticker price, net price and provides you with the tools necessary to estimate your out-of-pocket costs.

It is smart not to get too attached to a college until the financial aid packet is provided and students and parents can thoroughly assess their financial fit. The reality, however, is that future students can only determine their financial fit after the C/U accepts and provides them with their personalized financial aid letter.

Therefore, after your teen submits their application, colleges will let you know if they admitted your teen. Those that did accept them will provide a financial aid letter. This letter will include specific financial aid information on how much aid a college offers to entice your teen to commit and enroll.

These financial aid award letters are typically provided within a few weeks after the acceptance decision. Also, it is important to note that your teen is not expected to make a decision to attend a college based only on the acceptance letter (the notable exception is when your teen applies Early Decision – more on that in Chapter 10).

Once you get that letter, you'll be able to determine your out-of-pocket costs for that college and then decide on financial fit. Until then, all the costs discussed in this section are estimates.

The next book in this series focuses on the financial aid letter, understanding its elements, determining your out-of-pocket costs, comparing colleges, and asking for more aid.

Here are two types of costs and values you need to pay attention to at this time:
1. The Total Cost of Attendance
2. The Net Price or the Out-of-Pocket Cost

1. The Total Cost of Attendance

Cost of attendance (COA) is the advertised price tag associated with attending the college for one year. The COA is commonly referred to as the sticker price. Many researchers refer to it as the sticker shock because it is typically higher than expected, and it can be a massive deterrent to applying to college. A 2021 study found that about 25% of parents of high school students and 38% of high school students expected one year of college to cost $5,000 or less.[26]

The total cost of attendance includes several elements: tuition, fees, room and board, books and supplies, transportation, and other expenses. The cost of attendance gets reported to various agencies, including the federal government, annually. In addition, college Navigator provides these values for the previous year. While this information is good to have, naturally, students and parents are interested in COA for the next academic year.

A college's website is the best source to find the COA for the following year. However, colleges often finalize this information either at the end of the fall semester or sometimes in spring. This delay is because many colleges may update their tuition, fees, or any component of the COA every year. In addition, vetting the COA may require several layers of approvals, including, in many cases, the college's governing boards. Throughout my career, I've seen colleges seek permission to increase COA between January and June, preceding the fall semester. In other words, let's say that your teen is a high school senior this fall and will be a college freshman next fall. You'll probably be able to learn the COA for your teen's freshman year next spring or later.

A college may increase tuition or other costs if it hasn't done so in a while. Plus, inflation may also prompt colleges to increase prices. While the timing of the increase is hard to determine, typical increases tend to start around 2%. Sometimes these increases impact only tuition, fees, room, board, books, or a combination of these categories.

That being said, most colleges provide the COA through the financial aid letter, if it has been finalized.

2. *The Net Price or Out-of-Pocket Cost*

Net price refers to the amount that students and their families need to pay for a year of college. Net price is also commonly referred to as the out-of-pocket cost. This amount can be covered by savings, income, loans, or other funds.

Each year financial aid officers build financial aid packages for students who get admitted by the university.

They do this using information from the financial aid applications (FAFSA, CSS Profile, or state). It is a vast amount of work. The officers then provide this information to prospective students through the financial aid letter. Many financial aid letters include gift aid (grants and scholarships) and loans.

The net price is the total COA minus gift aid (scholarships and grants). For example, if the COA for a college is $50,000 per year, and the student received $20,000 in gift aid and $10,000 in loans, the net price will be $30,000. Net price is highly dependent on the student, as each student may qualify for different types and amounts of gift aid.

I remember being blown away the first time I heard a college president mention that no two students pay the same amount at the same C/U. That happened at the beginning of my career. I was "green" then, and it was hard to imagine how that was even possible. But, it makes sense as no two students are eligible for the same amount of aid, and each student is packaged individually. In addition, many officers consider various elements such as grades, test scores, and information from financial aid application(s). Therefore, while the COA or sticker price is the same for everyone, the net price varies by student.

Each college reports the average net price for its students to the federal government annually. The net price reported to the federal government and published through College Navigator is for in-state/in-district students. In other words, a student planning to attend college in a different state than the one in which they reside, should not use the net price provided through College Navigator.

Determining the Cost of Attendance & Net Price

There are a few ways to look up the total COA and net price. We will focus on two of them:
- A. College Navigator
- B. Net Price Calculators

Before we get into details on how to learn the total cost of attendance using either one of these websites, let's open the Starter List and add two columns to it:
- "Cost of Attendance"
- "Average Net Price by Income"

College Navigator
The College Navigator website is one of the best sources of information about the COA and net price.

The Cost of Attendance. The nice thing about getting the COA from the College Navigator is how the information is provided. Expressly, the living arrangements, as well as the "other" expenses, are provided in three categories: living "on campus," "off-campus with family," and "off-campus" without family. Make sure you select the appropriate total expenses value.

Here's how to find the total cost of attendance information:
- Go to College Navigator - https://nces.ed.gov/collegenavigator/ and search by college name.
- Then go to the "Tuition, Fees, and Estimated Student Expenses" section
- Go to the Total Expenses section and look for the most recent and appropriate value for you, i.e., in-

or out-of-state by living arrangements – on campus, off campus, off campus with family.
- The amount included in the total expenses section covers: tuition and fees, room and board, books and supplies, and other expenses.
- Copy and paste the most recent "Total Expenses" value to the "Cost of Attendance" column in your Starter List.

Remember, these values are for prior years and may change slightly for the upcoming year. Here's the Cost of Attendance information provided through College Navigator.

The Average Net Price by Income. College Navigator also provides the average net price by income quintile. Here's how to get to it:
- Go to College Navigator - https://nces.ed.gov/collegenavigator/
- Search by college name
- Then go to the "Net Price" section
- Go to the Average Net Price by Income section and get the most recent and appropriate value. This option should be used only for private colleges or public colleges that someone would attend as an in-state student.
- Copy and paste the Average Net price for your income level into the Starter List.

Figure 7.3: Cost of attendance from College Navigator

TUITION, FEES, AND ESTIMATED STUDENT EXPENSES

ESTIMATED EXPENSES FOR FULL-TIME BEGINNING UNDERGRADUATE STUDENTS

- Beginning students are those who are entering postsecondary education for the first time

ESTIMATED EXPENSES FOR ACADEMIC YEAR	2017-2018	2018-2019	2019-2020	2020-2021	% CHANGE 2019-2020 TO 2020-2021
Tuition and fees					
In-state	$14,460	$14,460	$14,460	$14,460	0.0%
Out-of-state	$39,406	$39,766	$39,766	$39,766	0.0%
Books and supplies	$1,084	$1,108	$1,108	$1,154	4.2%
Living arrangement					
On Campus					
Room and board	$10,026	$10,322	$10,522	$10,522	0.0%
Other	$2,908	$2,972	$3,040	$3,094	1.8%
Off Campus					
Room and board	$10,026	$10,322	$10,522	$10,522	0.0%
Other	$2,908	$2,972	$3,040	$3,094	1.8%
Off Campus with Family					
Other	$2,908	$2,972	$3,040	$3,094	1.8%
TOTAL EXPENSES	2017-2018	2018-2019	2019-2020	2020-2021	% CHANGE 2019-2020 TO 2020-2021
In-state					
On Campus	$28,478	$28,862	$29,130	$29,230	0.3%
Off Campus	$28,478	$28,862	$29,130	$29,230	0.3%
Off Campus with Family	$18,452	$18,540	$18,608	$18,708	0.5%
Out-of-state					
On Campus	$53,424	$54,168	$54,436	$54,536	0.2%
Off Campus	$53,424	$54,168	$54,436	$54,536	0.2%
Off Campus with Family	$43,398	$43,846	$43,914	$44,014	0.2%

As you may recall, the Starter List – the Excel that you downloaded initially from College Navigator - includes a column with the Net Price. You can use that column as an estimate if you'd like, but I like the net price values available by income quintile more. So, here's the average Net Price information provided through College Navigator. Remember, these values are averages for in-state/in-district students.

Figure 7.4: Average net price by income quintile from College Navigator

⊖ NET PRICE

AVERAGE NET PRICE FOR FULL-TIME BEGINNING STUDENTS

Full-time beginning undergraduate students who paid the in-state or in-district tuition rate and were awarded grant or scholarship aid from federal, state or local governments, or the institution.

	2017-2018	2018-2019	2019-2020
Average net price	$16,227	$16,579	$16,655

Full-time beginning undergraduate students who paid the in-state or in-district tuition rate and were awarded Title IV aid by income.

AVERAGE NET PRICE BY INCOME	2017-2018	2018-2019	2019-2020
$0 – $30,000	$6,446	$6,686	$6,927
$30,001 – $48,000	$14,743	$15,197	$15,170
$48,001 – $75,000	$20,481	$20,696	$20,557
$75,001 – $110,000	$25,162	$25,389	$25,297
$110,001 and more	$27,210	$27,543	$27,534

Net Price Calculators

If your teen plans to attend a public college as an out-of-state student, the net price values provided through College Navigator will not be relevant.

With the renewal of the Higher Education Opportunity Act, in 2008, the federal government required each college across the nation to include a "Net Price Calculator" on its website. You can find it by searching for the *net price calculator* on the college's website.

Some calculators require more information than others. The vast majority of net price calculators also provide the estimated COA.

Keep in mind that the estimated net price provided through these calculators is not legally binding. Your net price or out-of-pocket amount may be slightly different from the one you'll get after your teen gets accepted (through the financial aid letter).

The net price calculators are not standardized, and there may be considerable variation between them. Some Net Price Calculators (NPC) may include scholarships and grants while others won't. For example, a student eligible for a Pell grant (awarded for demonstrated financial need) is likely eligible for it at all colleges, not just a few of them. However, some NPCs will not include this grant in the net price value. Similarly, some schools may ask for a student's GPA and test scores to calculate the net price, while others may not. Those that do may provide you with estimated gift aid and subtract that amount from the total costs to calculate the net price. Therefore, pay close attention to what types of gift aid are included in NPCs. The lack of standardization of NPCs can make net price comparisons across colleges challenging.

Some anecdotal evidence points to the fact that Net Price Calculators may provide estimated net prices several thousands of dollars lower than the net prices you'll get through the financial aid letter.

***

After intense research, my professional recommendation is to use College Navigator to get the sticker and net price values for public in-state and private colleges in your Starter List. Then use Net Price Calculators for the out-of-state public colleges in your Starter List.

For example, if you are a California resident and have a few CA public and private colleges in your Starter List, use College Navigator to determine the COA and net price. The costs are usually the same for private colleges, regardless of in-state or out-of-state residency. On the other hand, if you have a public college from Arizona on your list, use the Net Price Calculator. Use the "Type" column in the Starter List to determine whether a college is private or public.

***

Living On-Campus Requirements
Many colleges, especially those geared towards providing a residential experience, have living on-campus requirements. In essence, the school requires all freshmen, sophomores, or both, to live on campus. Some exclusions apply, and students who live within a certain distance from the college may be exempt from this requirement.

For example, let's say that your teen will attend a school that is 50 miles away from your home. But the college specifies on its website that all freshmen living more than 30 miles from the campus need to live on campus during freshman year. Hence your teen may be required to live on campus and will need to pay for room and board, or at least for room.

On-campus living requirements are typically established in response to research findings and college goals. There is plenty of student success research that points to the benefits of requiring students to live on campus, especially during the first year of college. Some of the benefits include a smoother transition between high school and college; getting good grades; proximity to classes, library, advisers, and faculty; developing good study habits and lasting friendships; and returning to college the following semesters and years, as well as being more likely to graduate from college.

Living on-campus requirements also align with the college's goals. Colleges invest lots of resources in their campus buildings, and filling up dorms tends to be important from the revenues perspective. All in all, living on campus benefits both students and colleges.

It should be noted that not all colleges that have dorms require their students to live in them. As we are going through college selection, what matters for now is that you have a good idea of these costs and plan for them. As you look up costs, keep this requirement in mind and double-check the college's website to learn what it entails.

***

One common question that I have had to address through my speaking, coaching, and corporate career has been – whether students should apply to colleges with a high sticker price. My answer has always been yes, for two reasons. First, most college students do not pay the sticker price. Put differently; most students receive gift aid (e.g., grants, scholarships) that decreases the sticker price. Second, a college applicant will learn how much college will cost them only after the college provides the financial aid information. This information, as we discussed earlier, arrives after the college acceptance. It is then the job of the student and their family to calculate the out-of-pocket costs and decide whether a college is a good financial fit.

***

So here's what my Starter List looks like after adding the total cost of attendance and the average net price by income. I set the income quintile to $48,000 – $75,000 to determine the appropriate net price for the in-state public and private colleges on my list.

Table 7.3: The Starter List with the cost of attendance, net price, and average net price by income quintile

Name	Type	Total Cost of Attendance	Net Price	Net price by Income
College 1	4-year, Public	$ 23,433	$ 14,610	$ 17,800
College 2	4-year, Public	$ 23,000	$ 12,568	$ 10,500
College 3	4-year, Private not-for-profit	$ 29,000	$ 23,103	$ 26,500
College 4	4-year, Public	$ 32,000	$ 13,502	$ 26,000*
College 5	4-year, Public	$ 31,000	$ 12,500	$ 28,000*
College 6	4-year, Public	$ 30,000	$ 10,904	$ 24,000*
College 7	4-year, Public	$ 21,200	$ 10,457	$ 9,000
College 8	4-year, Public	$ 30,000	$ 12,951	$ 26,000*
College 9	4-year, Public	$ 34,000	$ 11,361	$ 25,000*
College 10	4-year, Public	$ 31,000	$ 13,075	$ 23,000*
College 11	4-year, Private not-for-profit	$ 56,400	$ 24,020	$ 22,000
College 12	4-year, Private not-for-profit	$ 41,000	$ 33,420	$ 34,500
College 13	4-year, Public	$ 22,000	$ 9,857	$ 10,000
College 14	4-year, Public	$ 52,000	$ 23,562	$ 40,000*
College 15	4-year, Public	$ 23,000	$ 9,781	$ 18,000*
College 16	4-year, Private not-for-profit	$ 54,000	$ 21,696	$ 20,000
College 17	4-year, Private not-for-profit	$ 36,000	$ 13,254	$ 12,000
College 19	4-year, Public	$ 31,000	$ 14,559	$ 22,000*
College 20	4-year, Public	$ 33,000	$ 7,515	$ 8,000
College 21	4-year, Private not-for-profit	$ 34,000	$ 17,185	$ 16,000
College 22	4-year, Private not-for-profit	$ 36,000	$ 23,751	$ 22,000
College 23	4-year, Private not-for-profit	$ 39,000	$ 21,738	$ 23,000
College 24	4-year, Private not-for-profit	$ 36,000	$ 19,990	$ 21,000
College 25	4-year, Private not-for-profit	$ 60,000	$ 45,346	$ 51,000
College 26	4-year, Public	$ 30,000	$ 13,476	$ 25,000*
College 27	4-year, Private not-for-profit	$ 47,000	$ 20,612	$ 17,000
College 28	4-year, Private not-for-profit	$ 41,000	$ 19,843	$ 18,000
College 29	4-year, Public	$ 48,000	$ 20,823	$ 33,000*
College 30	4-year, Public	$ 24,000	$ 9,787	$ 10,000

*Indicates the Net Price for a public out-of-state college. Net price calculated using the Net Price Calculator. The rest of the values included in the Net Price by Income column were determined using College Navigator.
** Net Price - College Navigator.

Next, we'll focus on indicators that will help narrow down the Starter List and identify the colleges with the best academic and personal fit for your teen.

Chapter 8: Narrowing Down the List

We have added information related to the most critical features admission officers are looking for in future students. Now, let's shift our focus to student success information and then use it to narrow down our list to about ten colleges.

Again, most college selection processes tend to have an element of irrationality. My goal is to provide you with information that can assist you with making a significant life decision that may impact you and your teen's future.

By the end of this section, you'll learn everything you need to know about graduation rates and how to use them to identify your teen's likelihood of completing college in 4- or 6-years. You'll also learn about salary after graduation, licensure pass rates, and so on, and how these indicators can help inform your college selection process.

The Graduation Rate

The first indicator is the Graduation Rate (GR). It provides the percent of students graduating on-time (in 4 years) or later (5, 6, or 8 years) from the college they started at.

Let me start by saying that the graduation rate is complex and imperfect. Since its inception, everyone has had a bone to pick with it and what it measures. And the debate is far from over.

That has been because it is hard to understand, and many students are excluded from it. But, on the other hand, this imperfect and complex measure may become increasingly important when a college has a very low 6-year graduation rate.

The following section will help you determine what it means if it's relevant to you, and whether you may want to use it to inform your college selection.

Inclusions & Exclusions

One of the main criticisms associated with the graduation rates (GR) has been that it excludes many students. Here are a few scenarios that illustrate who is included and excluded from the GR calculations. Let's consider the following four students: Ann, Ben, Casey, and Dean. They all graduated from high school together and intended to pursue a bachelor's degree at College A. Ann and Ben enrolled in College A during the same fall semester. Ann registered for a full-time course load (typically 12 credits or more), while Ben registered for a part-time course load (11 credits or less). Casey decided to take time off and enroll in College A in the spring semester for a full-time course load. Finally, Dean decided to attend the local community college and then transfer to College A to complete their bachelor's degree.

Six years later, College A will report what happened to students similar to Ann. Given that graduation rates include only students who enrolled full-time during the fall, following their high school graduation, the GR calculations will only include Ann. Therefore, Ben, Casey, and Dean will be excluded from graduation rates calculations. Ben and Casey are excluded because the former did not enroll in college full-time and the latter because they did not enroll in college during the fall semester. Then, Dean will be treated as a transfer student and excluded from the GR calculation. In this example, only 25% of the students – i.e., Ann – will be included in the GR calculations.

Now let's expand on GR some more. Let's say that nine other students enrolled together with Ann – full-time during the fall semester, following their high school graduation. Six years later, College A reports the graduation rate for these ten students. Out of these ten students, three transferred to another college, two dropped out, and four completed their bachelor's degree in 4-years, while the remaining two completed their bachelor's degree in 6-years. Therefore, for College A

- the 4-year graduation rate is 40% as four students completed their bachelor's degrees in 4 years,
- the 6-year graduation rate is 60% because, in addition to the four students who completed their bachelor's degree in 4- years, two more completed it in 6-years, and
- the transfer-out rate is 30% as three students transferred from College A to other colleges.

These remaining three students will not be counted in the graduation rates of any college.

All in all, graduation rates will be relevant to you if your teen plans to enroll in college full-time the fall following high school graduation, similar to Ann. However, if your teen follows any other path (similar to Ben, Casey, or Dean), graduation rates will not be relevant for you and your teen.

The Difference between 4-, 5-, 6-, and 8-year Graduation Rates

Colleges must report their GR data annually. The GR information is tracked at three different points in time, at the
- 4-year mark (100% of the time required to complete a bachelor's degree or on-time graduation),
- 6-year mark (150% of the time), and
- 8-year mark (200% of the time).

The 6-year Graduation Rate is the Standard The vast majority of GRs that you will find through different websites or books tend to be the 6-year ones. Therefore, if you see a graduation rate without any specifications, it typically refers to the 6-year rate. For example, the Starter List of colleges that you downloaded from College Navigator provides a graduation rate; this is the 6-year rate.

The issue is that delays in graduation can translate into high costs to students. One study found that each extra year spent in college after the 4-year mark can cost students "an additional $469 per month in loan payments compared to if the student graduated" in 4-years. In addition, students who delay graduation cannot secure full-time jobs and may not be able to capitalize on all the financial benefits associated with a college degree. Studies found that costs associated with the inability to secure a full-time job "will generally be even larger than" college costs such as tuition or room and board. Therefore, delays in graduation "can have important financial consequences." The study recommended that parents and students pay attention to the 4- and 6-year graduation rates, especially when selecting colleges.[27]

The 4-year graduation rate can be an important indicator that can inform the college selection process. So, next, we'll add this data point to the Starter List of colleges.

Before we go forward, let's provide some perspective. The average 4-year graduation rates are around 45%[28] at the national level, and the 6-year graduation rates are around 63%.[29] In other words, out of one hundred students who enroll in college in a particular year, forty-five will graduate within 4-years, and eighteen more will graduate within 6-years from the college at which they enrolled as freshmen.

Now go to your Starter List and add a new column, "4-year Graduation Rate.".

Adding the "4-year Graduation Rate" to the Starter List

Graduation rates (GR) are available in College Navigator.

Here is how to find the 4-year graduation rate:
- Go to College Navigator and search for the colleges in your Starter List
- Go to the "Retention and Graduation Rates" section
- Scroll down to the "Bachelor's Degree Graduation Rates" section to find the most recent stats available for 4-year graduation rates
- Copy this value into your Starter List

Figure 8.1 illustrates how College Navigator provides the graduation rates information. Here is how to read it: out of all the students who started as freshmen full-time during the Fall of 2014, 66% graduated within four years, and 72% graduated within six years from the college or university where they started.

Figure 8.1: Graduation rates as provided by College Navigator

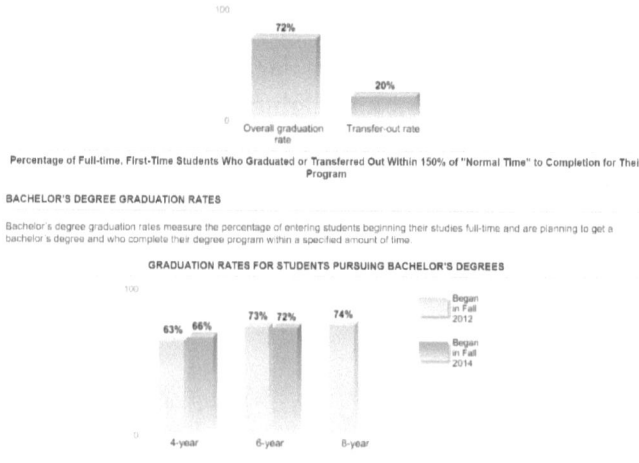

***

Before we move on to the next section, I would be remiss if I did not discuss several arguments related to graduation rates.

Selectivity & 4-year Graduation Rates

The first argument relates to "higher selectivity, higher graduation rates." It is argued that the more selective a college is, the higher its graduation rates. Figure 8.2 shows college selectivity and the 4-year graduation rate. Again you'll see that, of course, a handful of highly selective colleges have very high graduation rates. Still, you'll also be able to find many colleges with lower selectivity rates with high graduation rates. Therefore, don't get too stuck on selectivity rates as a significant predictor of on-time graduation.

As you evaluate Figure 8.2 remember that most high school graduates enroll at less selective colleges. A 2019 survey found that 80% of the freshmen students (first-time full-time, similar to Ann) enrolled in colleges that accepted 50% or more of their applicants (p. 9).[30]

A few findings become apparent once we use the 50% selectivity rate as the cutoff point. First, a lot of the "more selective" colleges (selectivity below 50%) have 4-year graduation rates higher than average, but also plenty of them have 4-year graduation rates below the national average. Second, about 58% of "less selective" colleges (selectivity rate at or above 50%) have 4-year graduation rates higher than the national average.

Test Scores & 4-year Graduation Rates

The second argument relates to "better students, better graduation rates." It is commonly argued that colleges that admit and enroll students with higher test scores will have higher graduation rates. Of course, colleges that accept students with the highest test scores out there tend to have the highest graduation rates. However, data show that only a few colleges admit students with the highest possible scores. The vast majority of colleges admit students with regular tests scores.

Figure 8.3 shows the 4-year graduation rate and 75th percentile in SAT test scores. As you can see, test scores and graduation rates are all over the place. Put differently, a student does not need a perfect score to find colleges with above-average graduation rates. In fact, data show that 61% of the institutions that reported test scores had 4-year graduation rates higher than the national average. In addition, the 75th percentile SAT score for some of these colleges and universities ranged widely, starting from 960.

Net Price & Graduation Rates

The third argument relates to the relationship between college costs and graduation rates. It is commonly believed that the more expensive a college is the higher its graduation rate. Figure 8.4 shows the average net price and 4-year graduation rates. As you can see, the values are all over the place. Sixty percent (60%) of the institutions had graduation rates above average, and their average net prices ranged between $6,000 and $44,000.

***

The data included in these figures (8.2, 8.3, and 8.4) represent the selectivity rate, test scores, and net price, respectively for the group of students (similar to Ann) who started college in the Fall of 2014 and graduated from the same college four years later. These data are freely available, provided by the National Center for Education Statistics through IPEDS.

This is all to say that smart college selection, can increase future students' probability of completing college in 4-years with the least amount of debt.

I added the 4-year graduation rates for all the colleges on my list. Here is what my Starter List looks like now – Table 8.1.

Figure 8.2: Selectivity and 4-year graduation rates

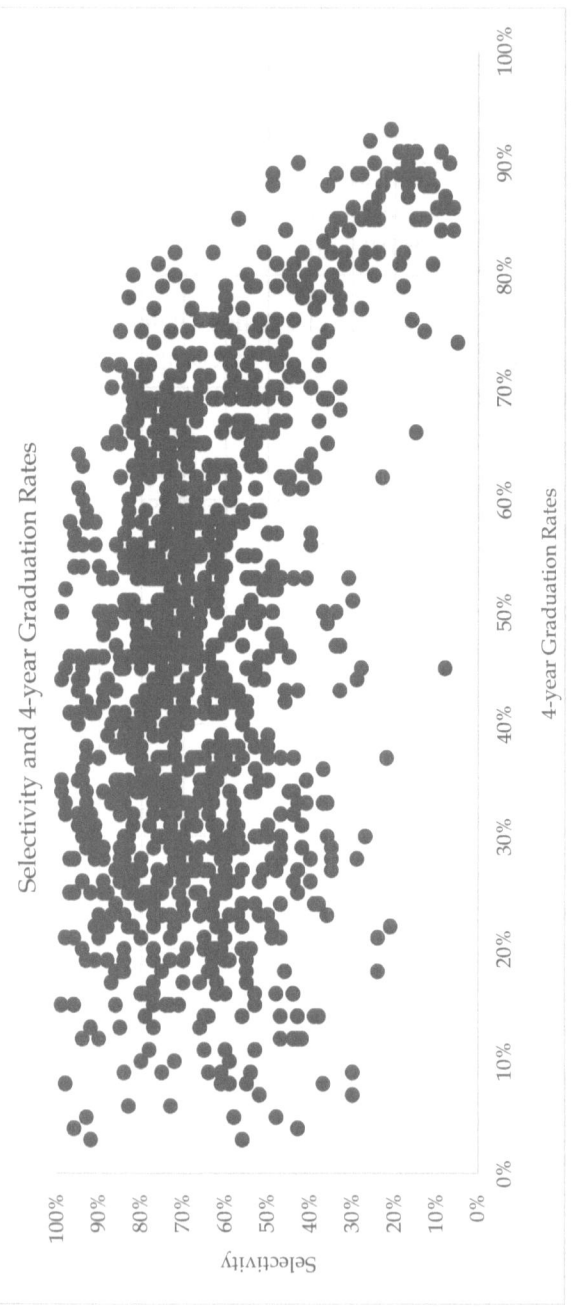

Figure 8.3: The 75th percentile SAT score and 4-year graduation rates

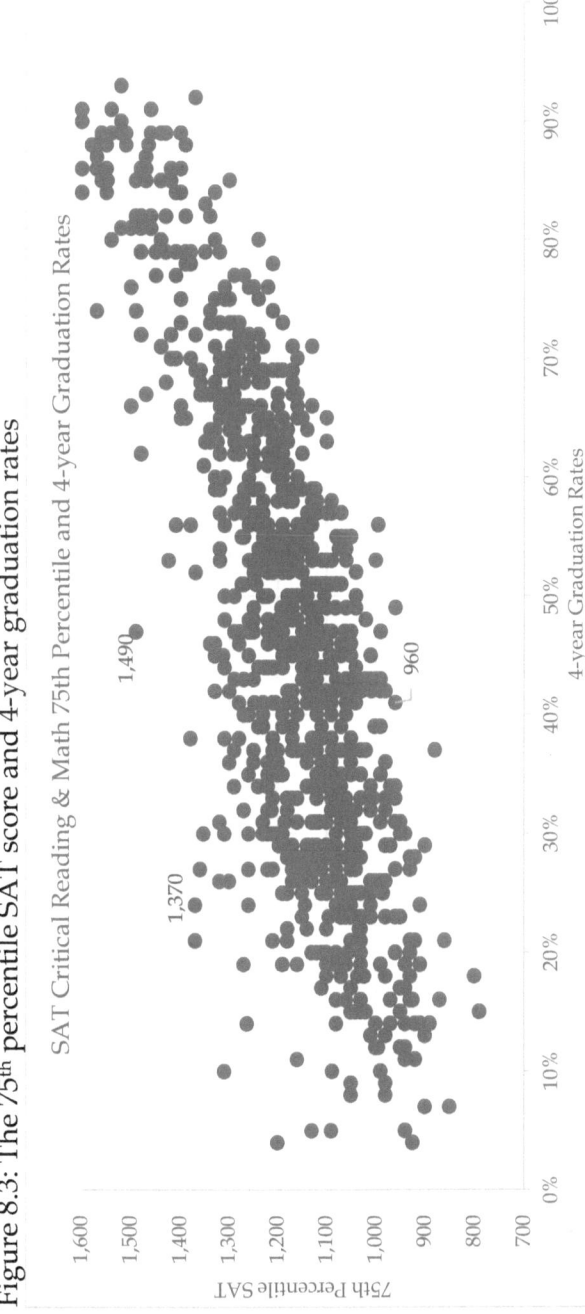

Figure 8.4: Average net price and 4-year graduation rates

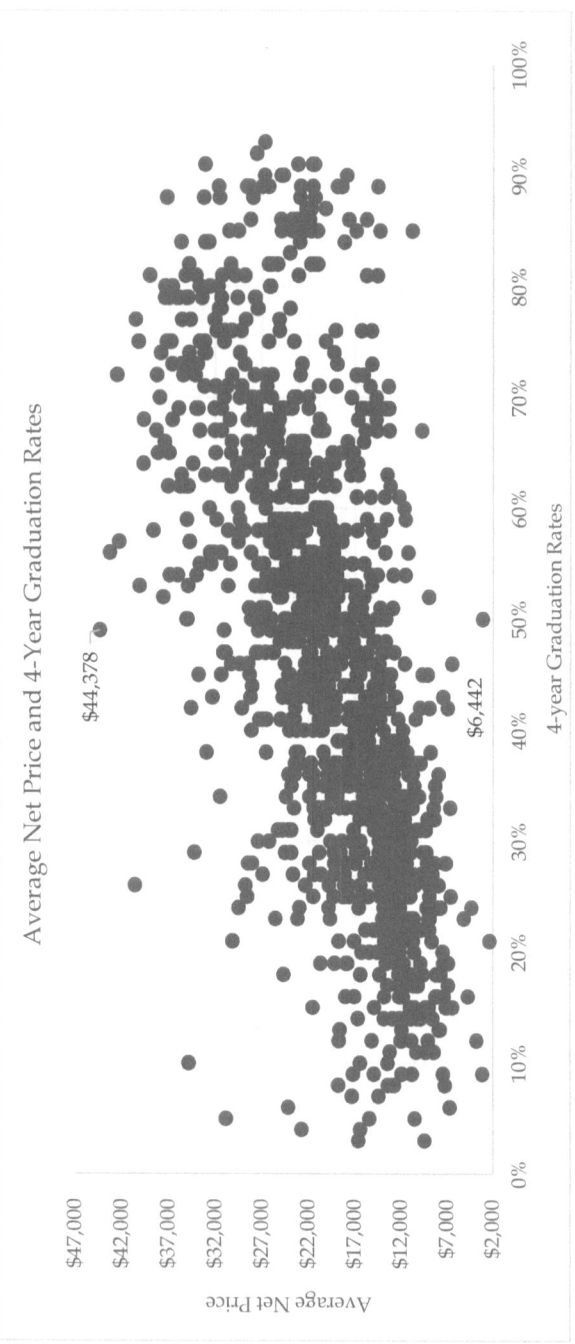

Table 8.1: The Starter List with the 4-year graduation rates

Name	Avg. HSGPA	Avg. HSGPA Determination	Testing Policy	SAT 25th-75th Percentile	Standardized Testing Determination	4-year Graduation Rates	Graduation Rates (6 year)
College 1	3.47	Safety	Required	1,030 - 1,160	Safety	22%	53%
College 2	4.07	Dream	Optional	1,200 - 1,340	Dream	68%	83%
College 3	not found		Optional	670 - 900	Safety	11%	47%
College 4	3.07	Safety	Blind			18%	40%
College 5	not found		Optional	668 - 890	Safety	12%	23%
College 6	3.27	Safety	Required	940 - 1,120	Safety	19%	38%
College 7	4.5	Dream	Blind			67%	88%
College 8	3.37	Safety	Required	930 - 1,090	Safety	25%	47%
College 9	2.96	Safety	Required	860 - 1,100	Safety	15%	38%
College 10	3.29	Safety	Optional	850 - 960	Safety	11%	35%
College 11	3.53	Safety	Blind			40%	52%
College 12	3.24	Safety	Blind			29%	52%
College 13	3.91	Reach	Optional	1,090 - 1,260	Reach	35%	67%
College 14	3.9	Reach	Required	1,150 - 1,320	Reach	51%	79%
College 15	3.27	Safety	Blind			10%	23%
College 16	3.86	Reach	Blind			51%	66%
College 17	not found		Required	940 - 1,120	Safety	42%	50%
College 19	3.58	Safety	Blind			9%	34%
College 20	3.22	Safety	Blind			25%	46%
College 21	3.49	Safety	Optional	880 - 1,110	Safety	22%	28%
College 22	3.43	Safety	Blind			41%	53%
College 23	3.26	Safety	Blind			41%	49%
College 24	2.8	Safety	Required	1,000 - 1,160	Safety	15%	33%
College 25	not found		Blind			45%	68%
College 26	not found		Optional	880 -1,020	Safety	16%	33%
College 27	3.13	Safety	Optional	1,000-1,148	Safety	36%	41%
College 28	3.47	Safety	Blind			32%	49%
College 29	3.98	Dream	Optional	1,110 - 1,260	Safety	49%	64%
College 30	not found		Blind			60%	75%

Narrowing Down the Starter List

Now is the time to narrow down our Starter List of colleges.

So here is how I went about it:
1. I sorted my Starter List by 4-year GR in descending order so that the colleges with the highest GR are at the top.
2. I picked about six colleges with the highest GR for each category of Dream, Reach, and Safety.

I ended up with 18 colleges to research further. But you may end up with about 15 to 20. This is not to say you should not research the other colleges in your Starter List. But if you are pressed for time, focus your efforts on these 15 to 20 colleges first.

***

The following section includes several other indicators that you could use to research your colleges further.

Feel free to use as many indicators as you'd like to narrow down your Starter List and identify the list of colleges to apply to. You may want to use only one or several of them; it is entirely up to you.

This is where the rubber meets the road. After you have all these data in one place, you'll be able to make some decisions that may impact the course of you and your teen's lives.

Remember, you and your teen can always go back and add colleges to the Starter List whenever you need to, and as many times as you need to.

Salary after Graduation and Median Earnings by Field of Study

The College Scorecard is another important data aggregator, maintained by the U.S. Department of Education. It provides students with valuable information in an easy-to-read and understand manner.

Some of the newest data points include salary after graduation and median salary by field of study. While it notes on its website that the "U.S. Department of Education cannot fully confirm the completeness of these reported data," these data are a significant step in the right direction. In time this data will become more and more complete and highly informative. In the meantime, know that this information is available and can provide information on potential earnings after graduation.

This data can also be an excellent indicator of how much debt a student should take on for a college degree. The rule of thumb is that the total amount of debt students should take on for the entire duration of college should not exceed their first or second year's salary. So, for example, if a student plans to pursue a bachelor's degree in accounting and the average wage at College B two years after graduation is $52,000, the student and their family may want to limit the borrowing amount to no more than $52,000 for the entire bachelor's degree at College B.

Programmatic or Discipline Accreditation

Another area of interest that may inform your college selection process is accreditation information. If your teen plans to pursue a program overseen by an accreditation agency, check out the program's accreditation status.

Programs such as Business, Nursing, Dietetics, Education, Engineering, Health, and others tend to be overseen or regulated by specific accreditation agencies. To determine if a discipline accreditor accredits your program, check out the Accreditation section in College Navigator.

Licensure Pass Rates

Some disciplines and states require that graduates pass a licensure exam to work in the field. Nursing is one of these disciplines. The licensure exam for Nursing is called NCLEX. If your teen plans to pursue a Nursing degree, you may want to check the NCLEX pass rates for the college.

Students who become familiar with the pass rates for first-time test takers (college graduates who took the exam for the first time) will very likely benefit from this information.

These values are available through a state's Boards of Nursing or directly from the college. So, first, find out if your state has a Board of Nursing and look on its website for this information. Alternatively, check out the college's website or email the Dean of Nursing and ask for this information. While getting this information may not be straightforward, getting it at this point may be extremely helpful to inform your college selection process.

The College Visit

This is a great time to talk about the college visit. College visits are one of the best ways to determine personal fit with a college. In addition, research has found that students choosing to attend a college based on the experience from a college visit were more likely to persist through college and graduate (p. 25).[31]

The pandemic ushered in a new era when it came to college visits. Many colleges adapted to the new reality by getting students acquainted with the college and its campus using alternative methods. Some colleges started providing virtual tours, small group visits, drive-through tours, or opportunities to interact with students and faculty over the Internet.

There are two best times to visit a college - before applying and/or after you receive the financial aid award letters.

Some of the main benefits of visiting the campus early in the admission process are that it can (1) power up the search and get your teen excited about the whole process and (2) help them decide if they'd like to apply.

There are benefits to visiting the campus later on as well. After getting accepted and receiving the financial aid award, you and your teen can visit the college. Then you'll have a clear idea of how much it will cost to attend for the first year. Additionally, visiting the campus now will help you determine if you'd like to negotiate your financial aid packet. As you'll see in The Ultimate College Financial Aid Guide book, you can appeal or negotiate your financial aid packet. However, I only recommend it for students committed to attending a specific college. This is because negotiating the packet of financial assistance takes a lot of planning and effort both on your side and the college's side. Therefore, this visit will help you determine your next steps.

Some typical activities for in-person visits include a tour of the campus, an information session, and some time to explore the campus and facilities. In addition, spending a few hours on campus may provide a good idea of the campus and the college.

Virtual visits typically include an information session, a virtual tour of the facilities, and live conversations with current students or faculty. You may even be able to attend a virtual class. It all depends on the college.

Each campus schedules its campus visit activities in its own way. Make sure you check the website to learn more and register for various activities.

Either virtual or in-person, make sure you take notes. On the one hand, you should note all the unique features and strengths of the college. On the other hand, jot down your feelings regarding the presentation, visit, campus, facilities, students, and faculty, especially if you are lucky enough to attend in person. These notes will come in handy when you have already visited a few campuses and have difficulty remembering the specific features of each college.

Other great benefits of college visits include application fee waivers. Some colleges may waive the application fees for students who visit the campus. Plus, some colleges may also offer discounts for the first year for students who visit the campus. So, be on the lookout for these.

Do your homework before the college visit. Make sure you are familiar with the college's history, values, and, if possible, priorities. This will help you understand your fit with the college and the college's fit with you.

As you plan your college visit, make sure you schedule it sometime during the fall or spring semester. This way, you will have a chance to meet with students and faculty and ask them questions about the college. If you are lucky, you may be able to find students and faculty in your desired program. Then, you can ask them about the courses in the program, the expectations of the faculty, and program requirements – such as internships, prerequisites, core courses, tutoring, counseling, and career advising.

Overall, visiting a college before or after getting accepted can help students decide if the college is a good fit. Vising the college before applying will help students determine personal and academic fit. While visiting after receiving the financial aid letter will help students determine financial fit, in addition to the personal and academic fit.

Student Support Services

Student support services are an essential component of the college experience. They may include career services, advising, tutoring, library holdings, and counseling. These services may be essential, and all students benefit from them, especially the undecided ones.

Make sure you do your homework and learn as much as you can beforehand. Then when you and your teen visit the campus – virtually or in person - make it a point to visit the career center. You may be able to talk to some staff in the career center, or maybe even the director. In my experience, career center staff are always happy to speak to current or future students.

Another important stop during the college visit is advising. First, you'll want to know what kind of academic advising services are available—for example, navigating program requirements, deciding on a major, changing majors, or determining the course load for the upcoming semester. So it is helpful to know the academic advising services and who staffs them. Some colleges have professional advisers, others have faculty advisers, and some have a combination of professional and faculty advisers. It is common for a college to have professional advisers for the freshman and sophomore students and faculty advisers for junior and senior students. Knowing this information may help inform your college decision process.

Plus, as a follow-up to this, you may want to ask about mentoring opportunities. Ask admission staff or academic advisers whether the college has mentoring programs. Some colleges have upper-level students mentoring first-year students. Other colleges may have faculty and staff mentor students. Figure out which model your teen would enjoy most and use that information for the college decision.

As you and your teen are on campus, try to spend some time in the library. Observe the layout, resources, computer labs, study spaces, etc. Talk to the library staff and ask them if individual or collaborative study spaces are available and how students can reserve them. This will come in handy in the future. For example, if your teen lives in the dorms and needs some quiet study time, they'll know how to go about reserving it at the library. Plus, these study spaces will come in handy for group projects. The college experience is filled with group projects, so knowing that students can reserve a room for them and their team when needed will come in handy.

When at the library, make sure you ask about tutoring services. Tutoring services tend to be housed and managed by the library. Ask what kind of tutors are available and how students go about scheduling tutoring sessions. This will come in handy later on when homework is due.

Finally, make sure to ask about counseling services. College is the first time when young adults are away from home, and they are bound to encounter some adjustment challenges. Having someone to talk through these adjustments will help students transition and acclimate to the new academic standards and college life overall.

Other Research Areas or Factors

Student-to-Faculty Ratio. The student-to-faculty-ratio tends to be a measure that has received a certain level of attention in relation to college selection. It refers to the average number of students associated with one faculty member. The value is calculated by dividing the total number of undergraduate students (freshman, sophomore, junior, and senior) by the total number of faculty teaching at the undergraduate level. This ratio does not mean that all the classes are small or that your teen will end up in smaller classes. In fact, due to their introductory nature, freshman and sophomore classes may end up being quite large, even though the ratio may look low. College Navigator provides this information by school. Search for your college in College Navigator, and you'll find the ratio in the header section.

Experiential Learning. Experiential learning has become popular during the last few years. It developed in response to college engagement research and job market demands.

In an effort to help students experience a seamless transition between college and work-life, colleges structured internships, co-ops, research courses, study abroad, leadership experiences, and so on. They put them all under the experiential learning umbrella. While internships, co-ops, and so on have been available to some extent in the past, the advent of experiential learning has structured these options. Moreover, experiential learning ensures that each student pursues at least one of these opportunities before graduating from college.

Go to the college's website to learn more about the experiential learning opportunities it offers.

Selectivity & Rankings. As you are reading through these factors, you may be wondering how come we didn't touch on selectivity and rankings yet. So here are a few things to keep in mind.

Selectivity. Selectivity or acceptance rate measures how many of the students who applied got accepted.

Selectivity is an indicator that is easy to use and understand. This may explain why so many people get hung up on it. The issue is that selectivity is easy to influence and does not provide the entire picture of college quality.

In a *Washington Post* article in 2017, Jeffrey Selingo explained how colleges influence selectivity and rankings. He noted that colleges "buy more than 80 million names of test takers from College Board annually." Colleges then encourage students from these lists to apply and hence drive up the number of applications while at the same time accepting about the same number of students every year.[32]

Additionally, a 2018 Stanford study found no relationship between a college's selectivity and "student learning, future job satisfaction, or well-being." The study did find a modest relationship between "financial benefits and attending a more selective college, but these benefits were found to "apply more to first-generation and other underserved students." It concluded that "individual student characteristics (such as background, major, ambition) may make more of a difference in post-college outcomes than the institutions themselves" (p. 1).[33] Finally, the study found "no evidence that students' learning will suffer for attending a less selective college" (p. 11).[34]

All in all, if selectivity is important to you and you'd like to learn the most recent value go to College Navigator, enter the college name, and then go to the Admissions section. If the college is not open access, it will list the acceptance rate in the Percent Admitted line.

Rankings. In terms of rankings, a 2018 article from *Inside Higher Ed*, citing the same Stanford study, noted that "the best way to find a college that is a 'good fit' is to ignore the rankings."[35] This study examined each criterion included in the rankings and researched factors such as "student learning, well-being, job satisfaction, and future income." The study concluded that if students and parents cared about these factors, then "the rankings will not steer [them] well."[36, 37]

Plus, that same Stanford study found that while parents and students look at rankings as indicators of quality, "the metrics used in the rankings are weighted arbitrarily and are not accurate indicators of a college's quality or positive outcomes for students" (p. 1).[38] Additionally, "there are better ways to choose a college than to rely on rankings, and especially selectivity as the main criteria" (p. 9).[39] On the other hand, the study found student engagement "more important than where" a student attended. Students who participated in internships had mentors who encouraged "them to pursue personal goals." Students who "engaged in multi-semester projects" were found to be "more likely to thrive after college" (p. 1).[40]

Finally, the study notes that "students should look at much more meaningful characteristics than selectivity and rankings when" deciding where to go to college (p. 18). Additionally, "rather than choosing a school based primarily on a flawed scoring system, students should ask whether they will be engaged at the college in ways that will allow them to form strong relationships with professors and mentors, apply their learning via internships and long-term projects, and find a sense of community" (p. 18).[41]

Taken together, these factors mentioned by the Stanford study and the ones included in this chapter may be more relevant to informing the college selection process.

***

Now is an excellent time to take a moment and decide which ones of these additional factors are essential for you and your teen. Then, pick one or more and add the information to the list.

Students and parents may want to select colleges using the information from the college visit, or maybe earnings after graduation, especially if students have a clear idea of what they'd like to major in. Alternatively, students and parents may want to choose colleges with strong student support services (advising, tutoring, counseling, career center, and so on), especially when students are undecided. That way, they'll have all the help they need to find the major that fits them best.

There is no right or wrong way to go about it. After you select these additional factors to narrow down your list, you should end up with a list of about 8 to 10 colleges. Plan to keep a fair number of Safety, Reach, and Dream colleges on your list.

Keep your focus on the best academic, personal, and financial fit. All in all, your teen should be pretty happy attending any one of these colleges should they get admitted.

Chapter 9: Preparing the Essay

I have debated intensely whether to include the college essay in this part or the college application part. Finally, I decided to include it here for the following reasons:

1. The college essay will probably be the most time-consuming activity associated with the college application.
2. The best time to start working on the college essay is at the end of the junior year. Therefore, if you have a chance to read this part during junior year, you are in great shape to prepare a great essay and college application.
3. Life will likely become quite intense once college applications open on August 1st. Having the college essay (almost) completed by then will help. There will be plenty of materials you and your teen will need to gather together to prepare a great college application and submit it before the deadline.

Again, the best time to start working on the college essay is at the end of the junior year, but the next best time is whenever your teen has a chance to do it. As you'll learn next, starting is usually the biggest hurdle.

The Common Application (CommonApp) is a college application portal that allows students to apply to more than 900 colleges. We will discuss the CommonApp extensively in Chapter 11. But, for now, we'll focus on it from the perspective of essays. The CommonApp provides the essay topics used by colleges when evaluating applicants for college admission.

Typically, CommonApp publishes these prompts in January, when high school juniors are getting ready to start the college admission process. As you'll see, these prompts provide considerable flexibility and may change slightly over time. To see the latest essay prompts, please visit:
https://www.commonapp.org/blog/2022-2023-common-app-essay-prompts

It is always good to review the admission requirements listed on college websites to identify the essay requirements and prompts. That is because most colleges that are part of CommonApp accept essays based on prompts from CommonApp. But some colleges have their essay prompts. Finally, I should also note that some colleges do not require essays; this seems to be the case for California State Universities. [42,43]

Now that you know whether your college requires an essay and its prompts let's focus on the features of a successful essay. An essay expert has written this chapter. Ms. Laurie Knitter has been an English teacher for more than 30 years and has reviewed and provided essay feedback to many college applicants.

While the remainder of this chapter is mostly addressed to teens, it provides parents with a great understanding of the requirements associated with the essay and a way to evaluate their teen's essays. Because parents are usually the first reviewers, therefore, knowing what to expect and what's required will empower you to help your teen develop their best essay.

How to Prepare a Successful Essay

An online search of the phrase "how to write the college essay" results in loads of websites listing tips and examples. The ones I read looked reasonable – be concise, proofread, be interesting (awful word—too vague, overused, and meaningless). That's good stuff. What is it, however, that sets the truly great college essay apart from the merely adequate? The answer is simple. It's you. It's *your story* that will set your essay apart from all the others and get you that coveted spot on the acceptance list of your first-choice college or university.

College admissions officers need to know who you are to determine if you are a good fit for their schools. So you need to tell them your story. By 'your story,' however, I don't mean the entire story of your life. What I mean is that you need to tell a story about an incident or time in your life that has had significance to you. It could be as unique as volunteering for a summer with Doctors Without Borders, or it could be a quieter piece reflecting on the bond built with a grandparent over repairing a screen door. Your story, to be effective, must have significance to you, and you must convey that significance to a college admissions officer.

Of course, college admissions officers want to see if you can write an adequate essay. You know the drill – intro with thesis statement, well-structured body paragraphs, a conclusion that sums up the information. Admissions officers also know that students typically ask their English instructors to edit their papers before submission; therefore, grammatical blunders, garbled syntax, and massive typos shouldn't appear in any essay. It's a must, then, to ask a teacher, peer, or parent to review your writing. While a well-structured, concise (recommended 250-600 words), clearly written essay is expected, however, it's not your writing style alone that'll get you into that acceptance pile. It's the content.

The Common App essay prompts are not unusual: "describe an experience that changed you," "describe an idea that you have challenged and won," and so on. The prompt I'd like to address specifically, however, is the following: "Share an essay on any topic of your choice. It can be one you've already written, one that responds to a different prompt, or one of your own design." Why this one? Because it's a prompt that appears virtually every year on not only the Common App but in other school-specific applications as well. You can also answer this prompt well in advance of seeing any of the application requirements of your chosen colleges or even before you've even started research on which colleges might be for you and your teen. We've already talked about style; now let's get a closer look at content.

Tell me a story. From the time we are little children demanding a bedtime story to our adolescence and adulthood, we crave stories in books, films, television shows, and even video games. A streaming performance will only be binge-watched if it gives the audience a riveting story. But what story should you tackle? You can do some brainstorming with your friends, guidance counselor, teachers, and parents at this early stage. Remember, though; you need a story with a beginning, middle, and end. Don't just drone on for 600 words about how you're the tennis team captain, and you like tennis, and you're a really good captain (snore…). Instead, tell your reader about when your strings broke, and you had no substitute racket. How did you resolve this problem?

How do you write this riveting story, one that will get your reader to stick around to the end to see what happens? There is no one single way to accomplish this goal, but the first tactic I always tell my students is to start with a hook or grabber. Ask yourself, "What sentence can I write that will really grab my admissions officer's attention?"

Remember, these people have a limited amount of time to assess sometimes thousands of applications to narrow them down to a percentage that would be admitted for the incoming class. How will your essay stand out? How will an admissions officer distinguish between two students who have the exact same academic record, the same amount of extracurricular and leadership activities, and all glowing recommendations? The college essay may divide acceptances from rejections. Therefore, you've got to get your reader hooked. Now this isn't to say that an essay with perhaps a so-so first line can't be successful (see example below), but you need to try for that grabber.

Let's consider a couple of examples from my own experience—I'm one of those English teachers who have read a boatload of these essays in an almost three-decade career. Just last week, I read a marvelous essay that started with the line, "The summer before my junior year in high school, I found myself flying through the air and, in what seemed like negative time, landing on my head and cracking it wide open at the crown." While the sentence may not end up on the bestseller list, as a reader, I wanted to find out what had caused this awful event, how it is that this student is still alive, and what effects, if any, resulted from this accident. The student then used techniques of fiction to present his nonfiction story. He took us on his journey and *showed* us rather than *told* us what happened. Instead, he provided background (or exposition) setting the stage for the event (where and when), a bicycle accident. As a reader, I rode with him down the seemingly smooth lane until he saw some uneven pavement in the distance (rising action). He skidded into that pavement, became airborne, and landed on his head (climax).

The ambulance arrived (falling action), and the result of his injuries was revealed—a precipitous dip in his grades for the following semester (resolution). While the story sounds boring in my diagram of his paper, the writer's tone was suspenseful, and he created interest and intrigue by providing action verbs, plenty of reflection on his state of mind, and a horribly graphic, but effective, description of his wounds. As a reader, I not only wanted but needed to find out how this story ended. Note too, that this is a true story. Warning: be honest in your essay. If you say you led a team of youth scientists into the Amazon jungle for a summer to research a brand-new species of frog—that you discovered—you better have done it. The result's not pretty when colleges find out a student has lied on his or her application.

Here's another example of an opening line: "I woke up in the morning and I couldn't find any matching socks." I can imagine an admissions officer saying, "Great. I've got to read an essay by some immature 17-year-old whose worst problem is finding matching socks." The student who wrote this essay, however, was admitted to her first-choice college, which was a highly competitive school. I'd imagine that the admissions officer who read this essay thought as I did when I first read it. I knew that the student was academically talented, so this essay couldn't solely be about matching socks. I thought, "Let's stick with it to see where it goes." The gist of the story was that the student was in a hotel room when she couldn't find that sock mate and was almost late for a field trip with her classmates on a European tour. The field trip was to Auschwitz. The contrast between this seemingly shallow, privilege-revealing first line and this student's heartfelt reflections on her experience at the death camp gave this essay its power. The student changed on that field trip from a self-involved child to a reflective, empathic adult. That first line was deliberately dull—the student took a chance, and it paid off.

We've talked about style, content, and how to start the essay. Now let's look at a couple of more tips. Most students (most people really) have difficulty talking about themselves, but don't be self-defeating. In other words, do not put yourself down in the essay: "I'm not the smartest person in the class but…." You can honestly discuss your strengths without comparing yourself to anyone else. On the other side of the coin, however, don't be self-congratulatory: "I'm the best in my class at tidddlywinks." Boasting is a sure-fire turn-off. You need to sell your candidacy but maintain humility. The key here is not to compare yourself to others. Just talk about you.

Starting the essay is often the worst part of the process. You've just got to sit down and do it. In our English department, however, students have options in their junior and senior years for writing a college essay while fulfilling a course assignment. For example, in a course on modern fiction that I teach, students may write a short story based on any experience. It could be fiction, but if they want to use the story for their college essay, it must be true. Toward the end of the term in that same class, we read a novel called *The Things They Carried* by Tim O'Brien, which covers one soldier's experiences during the Vietnam War. I have students examine their own lives in an essay entitled "The Things I Carry."

These essays often bring out the student's fears and concerns and their strengths and interests and could form the basis for their college essays. Parents and students should contact their schools' English departments to see if opportunities to write the essay in courses are in place. However, whatever options are available, you should start putting pen to paper (or fingers to keyboard) during at least the second semester of your junior year. That's not to say the essay must be in perfect condition by then, but as I said, getting it started is always the most challenging part, so get it started as early as possible.

Admissions counselors want to know who you are. What makes you a better candidate for their school than Jasmine or Jane or Marty? Can you write a clear, concise essay? Do they get a sense of who you are from this essay? Have you told us a story that defines *you*? As I said earlier, with academic and extracurricular records being equal, what is it that will make one student's application rise above the pack? It's the college essay, of course.

Summary

Congratulations! You completed the first college admission milestone – identifying colleges with the best academic and personal fit.

By now, you have probably started researching colleges. Now you know what to look for in a college, you understand the value of casting a wide net and exploring all your options.

It may be very tempting at this point to think that there are only one or two colleges that your teen really wants to apply to and eventually attend. Therefore, why bother wasting time researching additional colleges now, as it may be better to forge ahead and skip the time needed for researching and finalizing the balanced list of colleges. But hear me out. First, admission into these one or two colleges is not guaranteed. Because of that casting, a wide net is important. Specifically, if your teen plans to apply under restrictive plans – Early Decision or Single Choice Early Action, they will receive the admission decision mid to late December. If your teen happens to be waitlisted or deferred, they will have very little time to research and prepare applications for other colleges, as many applications are due January 1st.

Second, even if admitted, you and your teen will want to be able to compare financial aid offers from multiple colleges before you commit to one. Getting more than one or two financial aid offers will help you and your teen determine financial fit. Then these offers will help you make an argument for asking for more aid from the college that your teen really really wants to attend.

By now, you know where to look for colleges, data, and how to balance your list of colleges. Therefore, spending a little bit of time researching and building a balanced list of colleges will save you from stress and last moment decisions. In the best-case scenario, you won't use it. In the worst-case scenario, you'll be ready to go if needed.

It would be best to work on this part at the earliest during the junior year. This is especially true for the essay. However, it is okay to finish it even later, during the fall of the senior year.

Plus, should your teen be on the fence about going to college and the winter break rolls around, and they finally decide that they'd like to go to college after all, this part can be completed then, too, albeit with fewer college options. So, start the process sooner, and you will have more control over it, more options, and experience less stress.

The next part discusses application plans, features, materials, and how to prepare financial aid applications.

Part III
COLLEGE APPLICATIONS

Now that we have the list of colleges let's focus on the applications section of the college admission process.

This part explores different admission plans. As you go through them, you'll understand them and be able to decide which one is best for you and your teen.

Then we'll discuss
- how to put together the applications,
- materials you should prepare,
- application fee waivers.

The last chapter of this part will focus on the ins and outs of financial aid applications. One important thing to remember is that many colleges may require financial applications to be submitted simultaneously or even earlier than the college application.

Now, let's get familiar with the most common admission plans colleges use.

Chapter 10: College Application Plans - The Alphabet Soup ED, EA, RD, RA, PA, …

Colleges are very innovative in their application processes. Colleges attract students and encourage them to send in applications in different ways. These ways to entice students to apply are referred to as application plans. Understanding the type of application plan(s) a college uses can provide applicants with a competitive advantage in the admission process.

We'll start the discussion of admission plans with the Regular Decision and then move on to the ones with earlier deadlines. The Regular Decision application plan typically has a deadline of January 1st. However, some other plans, especially Early Decision or Early Action, have November deadlines.

Many colleges use a combination of application plans. Some use Early Decision and Regular Decision, others Priority Admission and Regular Decision, or Priority

Admission and Rolling Admission. Remember, colleges have total flexibility as to which application plans or combination of plans to use. You may find colleges using a unique plan with some elements from the plans presented in this chapter. That's why after you read this chapter, make sure to check the admissions website for your colleges to learn your colleges' application plans, their unique features, requirements, and deadlines.

Before we get into more details about each application plan, it is worth noting that the sooner a student applies, the better their chances for securing gift aid. Therefore, should your teen finish college applications earlier than the stated deadlines, encourage them to submit them.

Here is the list of the most common application plans that we'll discuss in this chapter:
- Regular Decision/Application (RD)
- Early Decision (ED)
- Early Action (EA)
- Single Choice Early Action (SCEA)
- Priority Admission (PA)
- Rolling Admission (RA)
- Instant Decision Day (IDD)

By the end of this chapter, you'll (1) learn what different application plans mean and (2) be able to pick the best plan(s) for you and your teen.

The best time to read this section is after you have narrowed down your list of colleges. In the best-case scenario, you can read this during the summer before the senior year. However, if that is not an option, plan to read it no later than September of senior year, as some application plans have very early deadlines. It takes about two months to put together all the documents needed for a college application – Chapter 11 goes into more detail about how to prepare an application and what materials you'll need for it.

So let's dive in. The following section provides a brief overview of different application plans with pros, cons, and typical deadlines.

Regular Application/Decision (RD)

The vast majority of colleges/universities use this plan. Under this plan, applications are usually due January 1st.

Pros
- Students can apply to multiple colleges
- Accepted students have time to decide on a college and commit until May 1st
- Students can compare financial aid offers from multiple colleges

Cons
- Admission decisions arrive in March or April

Deadlines
- The application is typically due in early January
- Colleges provide admission decisions typically in March or April

Early Decision (ED)

Early Decision is a unique type of application plan. There are three critical features associated with it:

1. Students may only be able to apply to one early decision college, although the restrictions vary by college. [44, 45]
2. The admission decision is binding.
3. Students cannot compare financial aid offers.

A binding admission decision means that if the college admits the student, the student must enroll at the college.

Students who apply ED sign a contract through which they commit to attending the college if admitted. Students, parents, and counselors may also need to sign the ED contract. [46]

Pros
- Students gain early consideration for admission
- Students learn the admission decision typically mid-December - earlier than most college decisions

Cons
- The admission decision is binding – students who apply must enroll if admitted
- Students may only be able to apply to one college.[47] However, make sure to review college websites carefully, as applicants "are responsible for determining and following restrictions"[48] as it relates to early decision applications.
- Students cannot compare financial aid offers, as they receive only one offer
- Students whom the college has not accepted may have very little time to apply to other colleges

Deadlines

- Applications are typically due October or November
- Admission decisions are provided typically in December

Some colleges do a couple of rounds of ED, such as ED I and ED II. Students pursuing ED II typically need to submit their applications by early or mid-January. This application deadline overlaps with Regular Decision. Hence, through ED II, students typically can apply to multiple colleges. The ED II application is also binding, so if the student is accepted through ED II, the student commits to withdraw their applications from all the other colleges. Typically, students will get the ED II admission decision about a month later.

Use the ED options if:
- You and your teen have thoroughly researched the college, are absolutely in love with it, and are sure that your teen would attend if admitted
- your teen meets or exceeds the HSGPA and test scores of students accepted in the past
- you and your teen can afford the college with little or no gift aid.

In terms of acceptance, students who apply using the ED options tend to have higher acceptance rates. For example, a 2019 report noted that ED applicants had higher acceptance rates than the rest of the applicants – 61% vs. 49% - even though ED applicants represented only about 6% of the total applicant pool.[49]

Plus, due to its binding nature, the yield for the ED applicants was 90%. Remember, yield refers to the percent of students who enrolled in the college out of those who were accepted. The ED yield rates are substantially higher than the average yield rates for all students (25%) admitted by colleges using the ED plan.[50]

Admission officers put in hundreds of hours of arduous work reviewing thousands of applications, doing their best to determine if the students they admit are likely to attend. Then decision time comes around, and students choose to enroll somewhere else, so all that hard work was in vain. A way to mitigate against this is by using ED and taking a close look at students who already committed to attending the college when they applied.

In other words, colleges use ED because they like a commitment from the get-go. That allows a college to build its class earlier. If a college knows a student wants to attend, they are more likely to get admitted through ED than otherwise. Hence, the acceptance rates are higher for ED students.

It is important to remember that colleges use merit aid to incentivize students to commit to and enroll in a college. However, in the case of ED, students commit to attending a college at the time of application if the college admits them, no matter the cost. Hence, colleges may decide to forgo merit aid to incentivize students to attend.[51]

If a student needs a considerable chunk of gift aid to attend a college, then ED may not be the best way forward. Put differently, students who need gift aid to attend a college should consider other application plans.

While the ED contract is not legally binding,[52] colleges rely on students to honor their commitment to attend if accepted. On the other hand, admission officers have extensive networks. Therefore, they have the means to pursue students if they decide not to honor the ED contract.

Students can get out of the binding agreement because of the inability to afford the college.[53, 54] A student who asks for an ED release because of lack of affordability needs to hurry up and apply to other colleges through Regular Decision. In other words, the admission decision for ED tends to arrive around mid-December, and the financial aid offer may come a little bit later. If the offer of financial assistance does not provide enough aid to make it affordable, students need to regroup and apply to other colleges through Regular Decision or other application plans. Again, the timing is the issue because Regular Decision applications are usually due January 1st.

Therefore, make sure you know how much the college would cost ahead of time. If lack of merit aid would make the college unaffordable, you may want to reconsider using the ED plan. On the other hand, if you decide to pursue ED and the college's financial aid offer is unaffordable, be ready to ask to be released from ED and submit applications to other colleges by the Regular Decision (RD) deadline.

Meeting the RD deadline can be a bit daunting since, as you'll see later on, each college requires different materials in their applications, so gathering all these within a couple of weeks might be challenging. Therefore, it is wise to do your homework and have a thoroughly researched list of colleges in your back pocket, even if you and your teen decide to pursue ED. This list will come in handy if you need to explore other colleges and application plans. Another option for students who apply through ED and find the college unaffordable is applying to colleges using Rolling Admission plans (more details below). In other words, remember Universal Truth #4 – *you always have options*.

If ED is right for you and your teen, make sure you understand all the specifics outlined in the contract and don't stray from them. Keep in mind that some colleges are more particular than others when it comes to ED. Always check the college's website for the most up-to-date deadlines and requirements. [i]

Early Action (EA)

The Early Action (EA) plan provides more flexibility and a few more benefits.

Pros
- Students can apply to multiple colleges
- Students learn the admission decision usually in December
- Not binding - admitted students can decline the offer and choose to attend another college
- Admitted students can compare financial aid offers from multiple colleges and usually have time to decide and commit to a college until May 1st

Cons
- None

Deadlines
- Applications are typically due in October or early November

- Colleges provide admission decisions typically in December

The 2019 NACAC report found that EA applications represented 45% of the total applications for colleges that offered EA admissions. The admission rate or selectivity for EA applicants was 73%, versus 64% - the overall selectivity for all applicants. In terms of yield, the enrollment rate for students accepted through EA was similar to the yield for the rest of the applicant pool (25% vs. 24%).[55]

In other words, the probability of acceptance increases slightly for students applying through EA. This plan may be relevant in the context of students being able to apply early to multiple colleges simultaneously and being able to evaluate various financial aid options. Plus, EA students can choose which college to attend, as EA is not binding, like ED.

Restricted Early Action or Single-Choice Early Action

This model combines ED and EA. While very few colleges use this model, those that do tend to be very prescriptive. Check the colleges' websites to learn the details and terms associated with this model. Here is some general information about this model.

Pros
- Admission is not binding
- Students gain early consideration for admission and learn the admission decision typically in December

- Students usually have time to decide and commit to a college until May 1st
- Students can compare financial aid offers from multiple colleges

Cons
- Students can apply to other colleges, but each college is very prescriptive as to which other colleges students can apply

Deadlines
- The application is typically due in November
- Decision notifications vary by the college but tend to be provided earlier than March

Priority Admission (PA)

Some colleges use the priority admission model. These colleges tend to use it to provide students with early admission and merit aid consideration.

Pros
- Students can apply to multiple colleges
- Students may learn the admission decision earlier
- Students may get considered for merit aid sooner than the ones applying through Regular Decision
- Accepted students usually have time to commit to a college until May 1st
- Students can compare financial aid offers from multiple colleges

Cons
- None

Deadlines
- Applications are typically due October or early November
- Colleges typically provide admission decisions in February

Rolling Admission (RA)

A large number of colleges use this plan. It provides students with significant flexibility. Colleges consider students when they apply – in other words, first come, first served. Therefore, the sooner students apply, the better their chances for admission and financial aid.

Pros
- Students can apply to any college at any time after the college/university starts accepting applications. In some cases, it may be as soon as August or September (of senior year) and, as late as the beginning of the fall term (freshman year), provided that the college is still accepting applications
- Colleges review applications as soon as they receive them
- This is an excellent option if you want to complete the college admission process early or haven't found a good academic, personal, and financial fit yet. Additionally, it may be an excellent option for students who were on the fence and missed all the application deadlines but decided that they did want to go to college after all.

Cons

- Gift aid (scholarships and grants) tends to be awarded first-come, first-served.
- The sooner you apply, the better your chances at securing gift aid.
- Colleges have a limited number of students they can admit for the fall term. The sooner you commit, the likelier you are to secure a fall class spot.

Deadline
- There is no deadline for the application
- College decisions are typically provided quite soon after the student applies

Instant Decision Day (IDD)

Instant Decision Day events are typically held at high schools. College representatives go to the high school, interview students and provide an admission decision on the spot.

Pros
- It eases the pressure on the students, as they may receive a college acceptance on this day
- Students can still apply to other colleges, hence the acceptance is not binding.
- Students can compare financial aid offers, provided that they apply to other colleges too
- Students get to sit down and talk with an admission officer and have a chance to explain their grades, activities and goals; they also have an opportunity to ask additional questions and learn about the next steps

- Students may need to meet minimum academic standards to be able to attend the event
- Many colleges waive the application fees for participating students
- Some colleges offer several Instant Decision Days each year
- Students who are not accepted can get feedback from an admission officer on how to strengthen their application

Cons
- Students may need to apply before attending the event

Deadline
- Applications may be due before meeting with college representatives, but it varies by college
- College admission decisions are usually provided on the spot [56]

***

While we have covered the most common application plans above, colleges are highly innovative. Some colleges may use a combination of these plans (i.e., ED and RD). Other colleges may combine elements of these plans and come up with their application plan. Sometimes this plan gets a name.

So by now, you may be wondering why colleges use all these application types. Well, here are some reasons for it. First, all colleges need to put together a great freshman class. The sooner they get students to commit, the easier it is. Hence, the ED, ED I, ED II, EA, and Priority options. As you may remember, most colleges cannot finalize their fall class by May 1st and may continue recruiting sometimes well into July.[57] Therefore, colleges need to entice students to apply and provide flexibility.

Second, selectivity has been essential for college rankings for a long time. Therefore, colleges have been casting a wider and wider net to entice as many students to apply, then reject them to increase their selectivity and consequently their ranking.[58]

***

Remember Universal Truth #4 - *you have options*. The college admission process is stressful enough as it is. Therefore, by knowing all your options, you can pick the best colleges and identify the application plans that best serve you and your teen, and confidently go through the admission process. Once you understand all our options, you gain control over the process and the stress subsides.

Chapter 11: The College Application

Now that we are familiar with all the application plans and deadlines let's discuss the mechanics of submitting applications. This section also focuses on the materials and time needed to complete college applications. Additionally, this chapter discusses application fees and fee waivers.

Parents and students would benefit most by reading this chapter before August 1st of senior year, as the college application season opens then. Alternatively, if pressed for time, plan to read it about two months before the earliest application deadline.

Application Platforms

Many colleges accept applications through various platforms. Here are some of the most common ways to submit a college application:
- The CommonApp
- The Coalition Application
- University Systems Applications
- College Specific Applications

The CommonApp

While we touched on it in the previous chapter, this section focuses more on the platform and how to use it to prepare and submit the college application.

About 900 colleges use the CommonApp www.commonapp.org. It allows students to enter all their information only once and apply to multiple colleges. In addition, it offers tutorials and details on colleges and academic programs.

Colleges can customize the CommonApp and often add additional questions, and supplemental essay prompts. Therefore, students need to plan for these additional questions and essays.

The CommonApp opens on August 1st, and students can apply as soon as they finish it.

If colleges in your list allow for submission through CommonApp, try to set up the account and review the requirements in early August. This will help you develop a system, start working through each college application's requirements and set up a timeline for putting together the materials for each application before the beginning of the senior year. [59]

Plan to allocate about two months to getting everything together and completing the applications.

The Coalition Application

Used by more than 100 colleges, this is another way to submit your application to colleges https://www.coalitionforcollegeaccess.org/. It is worth knowing that the opening date for the application varies by college, but "many Coalition applications for first-year students open in July and August." [60]

Some colleges that accept the Coalition Application also accept the CommonApp.

University System Applications

Some University Systems have their own college application platform. Therefore, students enter information only once and apply to multiple colleges in the system. At least two systems offer this option – the University of California System and the Texas System.

College-Specific Applications

It is important to note that while many colleges may accept applications submitted through any of these platforms, not all of them do. Some colleges require students to apply using the applications included on their websites.

***

Like everything else, each college has its way of dealing with applications. Visit the admission sections for each college to determine its application preferences.

Also, it is important to know that many colleges do not require students to use the CommonApp. Therefore, you can use whichever application option is best for you and your teen.

Make sure you read all the requirements associated with the application and answer all the questions. It is important to fill out even the information listed as optional, as colleges ask for it, and use it to understand their applicants better.

Each college can customize its application through CommonApp or Coalition. Hence, if you have questions it is best to contact the admission office of the college.

The Application Materials

Here's a Starter List of materials usually needed for the application.

Transcripts. Many colleges require transcripts with the college application. The transcript includes all the grades for all the classes that your teen took in high school.

The transcript will only include classes and grades up to the end of the junior year at the time of application. Colleges often make admission decisions using only this transcript. However, some may require the grades for the first semester of the senior year. Others may request the transcript for the entire senior year. Colleges can rescind admission decisions if grades falter during the senior year.

With the COVID pandemic and the shift to test-optional, many colleges started putting even more weight on transcripts. Therefore, make sure to submit them, so that they have all information they need to make a comprehensive evaluation and admission decision.

Also, plan to request your teen's transcripts ahead of time so that colleges receive them in time. Be mindful that seniors typically request these transcripts simultaneously, so processing them may take time.

Letters of Recommendation. Colleges typically require 1 to 3 letters of recommendation. Some colleges are quite particular about who should provide these letters – teachers, counselors, faculty members, coaches, employers, or advisers. Other colleges require letters of recommendation from English, Math, or Science teachers. Check the college's website to learn the requirements for each college.

It's best to request the letters of recommendation at the end of the junior year, as teachers and counselors will have the summer to write them. Alternatively, plan to ask for these letters at least 6 to 8 weeks before the earliest application deadline.

Teachers and counselors may decide to provide only a certain number of recommendations over the year. This is quite common, especially when many students ask for recommendations. Make sure your teen takes that into consideration and times their request accordingly.

It is always a good idea to request recommendations from teachers with whom your teen has had a good relationship, as they would be the best people to speak to your teen's personal and academic achievements.

The recommender usually submits letters of recommendation. Students using platforms such as CommonApp have a section to identify their recommenders and add them to the system. If the recommendations are required via postal mail, it might be good to provide recommenders with forms and stamped envelopes.

Some teachers may ask students to write the first draft of the letter of recommendation. Don't be surprised if this happens, as teachers tend to be slammed with recommendation requests. If students need to do that, they should give it their best shot and know that it will get edited, redrafted, and polished. From the recommender's perspective, it is sometimes easier to start with a draft than stare at a blank piece of paper, wondering where to start.

Teachers and counselors tend to be very busy, so it pays to always be kind, polite, and considerate with requests and follow-ups. I found that the most effective follow-up method has been through email, asking if they need any additional materials or information.

Writing letters of recommendation takes time, and teachers/counselors are not paid to write them. They do it because they believe in their students. Always thank everyone who wrote a letter of recommendation for your teen.

Resume. Some colleges ask applicants to submit a resume. Other colleges do not require it because they require most of the information through various application sections, which makes the resume redundant.

Developing a resume may help with the letters of recommendation. In addition, providing everyone a copy of your teen's resume and their plans for the future may make a recommender's job more manageable. That way, the recommender has all the information they need and can write more knowledgeably about academic and personal achievements and milestones. Try to keep the resume short, about one to two pages.

Scores. Many colleges moved to test-optional models, but some still require them.

When your teen takes the standardized tests, they can automatically send the scores to colleges.

Now you may face a dilemma–sending the test scores automatically or later on. If you choose the automatic option, sending the scores will be free, but you won't be able to see them before they are sent to the college. On the other hand, if you decide to wait to send the test scores until after you see them, you'll have to pay about $15 for each report you send to a college.[61]

If the college is test-optional, I recommend waiting to see how your teen scored. Once you have the scores, check how they compare with the 75th percentile values for students enrolled at the college in the past. Then decide whether sending the scores will enhance your teen's application.

It is quite common for students to take the tests three times or more. Colleges may have different policies as to which scores they will consider – i.e., all test scores from all dates, the highest test scores from all dates, etc. Check the website for the college's preference and decide how you'd like to go about submitting your scores.

Most colleges have no preference for submitting the SAT vs. ACT scores. Plan to send the test scores to colleges at least a month before the application deadline. Do this, especially for colleges that require them for admission consideration.

Extracurricular Activities. Some people will tell you to try to get into the mind of the admission officers and find out what activities they would like to see in their future applicants. Then convince your teen to pursue these activities, regardless of their interests, as these activities may increase their admission odds.

My take on picking high school activities is that aligning them with your teen's major areas of interest will pay off, including increasing college admission odds. In addition, your teen may want to align these activities with life goals, potential college majors, problems that they'd like to see solved in your community, or their plans. Plus, rather than picking every activity available, it is often better to pick a few activities and go in-depth.

It is beneficial for high school students to find out their passion(s), then get involved and delve deeper into activities that align with their passion(s). They may want to work their way up into leadership, coaching, or teaching positions, which will help their college application stand out. It is often more critical that students are true to themselves than second-guessing others' expectations. Plus, many college admission officers will tell you that authenticity goes a long way.

Another reason why I am advocating for your teen to identify and follow their passions and interests for selecting activities during high school is that college priorities often change. Remember the conversation from Universal Truth #2 – no formula will guarantee college admission. In that section, we discussed leadership and staff turnover. Therefore, second-guessing admission officers' preferences is unsustainable as officers and college priorities often change. In other words, it pays to pick activities that align with personal interests.

It is an excellent idea to keep track of these activities and awards, starting with freshman year of high school, include them on the resume, and curate them carefully for the college application. There's no need to have every activity in the application, but do try to find ones that tell a story about your teen. Plan to provide a brief description of each activity, how much time your teen devoted to it, and a brief explanation of their role. Plus, explain the problem your teen was trying to address and their contribution.

All in all, it is better to focus on including extracurricular activities that align with the student's passion, goals, and potential major or plans; rather than including everything or what students think may please college admission officers.

Supplemental essays. Colleges customize their applications to align with their goals and priorities. As a result, some of them include supplemental essays in the application. While many colleges list these essays as optional, it is always good to fill out these sections.

Make sure you walk through each college's application as soon as you set up your application account. Identify the requirements and optional elements for each college and start preparing the materials needed to fill out every component of the application.

Put differently, plan to provide supplemental essays even if they are listed as optional. Colleges use this information to get a better understanding of the applicant. Plus, in many cases, these supplemental essays can get applicants into the admitted pool. Hence, colleges gauge your teen's interest by the effort they put into completing these supplemental essays.

The CommonApp allows students to preview supplemental essay questions for their colleges before beginning their application through the "Student Solutions Center." [62]

The Financial Aid Application. A critical piece of the college application is the financial aid application. The next chapter discusses all the financial aid applications you may need to submit. Make sure you read the next chapter as soon as possible, as some financial aid applications may be due 2 to 4 weeks before the college application is due.

***

Overall, each college may be particular as to which materials it requires. Plan to provide information for everything the college lists as optional and required. Colleges usually use this information for admission decisions. Starting the college application early will give you enough time to identify what's needed for a successful application for each college on your list.

Application Fees & Waivers

Students must pay a fee to submit their college applications. This is a payment to the college. While not all colleges have an application fee, many do.

Application fees typically vary from $30 to $100 and are non-refundable. The admission section of the college website is typically the best place to learn more about the application fees. These costs can add up quickly, especially when students plan to apply to multiple colleges.

Under certain circumstances, colleges waive the application fee. Here are a few ways to get application fees waived.

High School Counselors or Officials. High school counselors often have the most up-to-date information about application fee waivers. Please make sure your teen checks with them before applying.

ACT or College Board. Students eligible to waive the test fees typically qualify for college application fee waivers. See more details:
- for College Board
  https://collegereadiness.collegeboard.org/about/benefits/college-application-fee-waivers
- for ACT
  https://www.act.org/content/dam/act/unsecured/documents/RequestForWaiverForm.pdf

CommonApp & Coalition Application. These application platforms allow students to request a fee waiver due to financial hardship. Your counselor will be notified and asked to affirm your request for a fee waiver. Plus, a number of colleges that accept applications submitted through these platforms do not have application fees. See more details for

- CommonApp https://appsupport.commonapp.org/applicantsupport/s/article/What-do-I-need-to-know-about-the-Common-App-fee-waiver
- Coalition Application https://www.coalitionforcollegeaccess.org/fee-waiver

College Waivers. Some colleges waive the application fees. They tend to do so for students who visit the campus or attend an online event. Additionally, sometimes colleges may send fee waiver codes through email. Make sure to check your email regularly.

In addition, some colleges waive their application fees during specific periods – a week or a few days. Be on the lookout for this and plan to submit your application then.

More importantly, colleges may waive the application fees if a student asks for a waiver. Your teen could reach out to the admission office with an email request.

Instant Decision Day. Students who attend the event have their application fees waived.

The National Association for College Admission Counseling. This organization provides fee waivers for students who meet specific standards. To learn more about this fee waiver, go to: https://www.nacacfairs.org/learn/fee-waiver/

Free Application Weeks/Days. In an attempt to encourage students to apply to college, several states provide free application days or weeks. For example, during October, states offer a few days or sometimes a few weeks, when high school seniors can apply to various colleges for free. If you plan to take advantage of these offers, make sure your teen has their applications ready to go around that time. This can save hundreds of dollars, which will come in handy later for other college expenses.

Seasoned high school counselors will have a very clear idea about your state's free application dates.

If your teen has questions about requesting a fee waiver, they should reach out to their high school counselors or the college.

Keeping Track of Everything

There are a lot of activities associated with college applications. Unfortunately, most parents and students need to complete these activities while super busy with the senior year. Plus, each college requiring different materials can further complicate the application process. But, know that life becomes significantly easier once the applications are submitted. So hang in there and complete the college application process as soon as possible.

It is wise to keep track of all the documents your teen submits to each college. Setting up folders for each college and storing all research, email exchanges, forms, application requirements, fees, the essay, and so on in the appropriate folders will help later on. Plus, these folders will help you manage all the application materials, and you'll be able to know what you sent in and what is missing from the application. Finally, the folders will help you refresh your memory when you need to determine financial fit.

Chapter 12: Financial Aid Applications

It is wise to start working on the financial aid application while waiting for the materials you'll use for the college application. Here are some reasons why this is the case.

First, many colleges may ask students to submit financial aid information early. They may use this information in the admission decision. Plus, some colleges ask that the financial assistance section be completed and submitted before the college application deadline – this is usually the case with the College Scholarship Service Profile (CSS Profile) application.

Second, many schools strive to provide future students with financial aid information simultaneously with the admission notification. Therefore, some students will learn about at least a part of the aid with the admission notification. This is the case, especially with merit aid. This is because admission offices have budgets they allocate for student recruitment. These funds are commonly referred to as institutional aid and are the first pot of money colleges can use to recruit students. There is typically no need for federal or state approvals to access these funds.

Plus, many colleges strive to provide students with financial aid information quickly. Colleges will often do their best to finalize the financial aid packages for the admitted students as soon as possible. This packaging requires intense effort as the financial aid officers must package all the students admitted and process the federal and state funds and institutional funds.

All in all, admission officers and college leaders have stringent internal deadlines for providing financial aid letters to students. Some deadlines ranged from five business days to several weeks after sending the admission notification. Hence, the timing of the offer of financial assistance varies by college.

On the other hand, colleges understand how stressful the college admission process is. They know that providing you with the financial aid information can help you narrow down your list of colleges, weigh in your options, and, in some cases, commit to the college and pay the deposit. Once you do that, they finalize adding a student to the incoming class. One admission officer explained it this way: how nice would it be to know that you wrapped up the college admission process before Christmas, and you can now enjoy the holidays and the rest of the senior year. While this is a significant achievement, please don't feel pressured to rush the college decision.

It is always a good idea to weigh your options carefully and find the college with the best academic, personal, and financial fit. Be flexible, keep an open mind and take your time deciding. The reality is that you can identify the college with the best financial fit only after receiving offers from a few colleges and calculating the out-of-pocket costs for each one of them. Then you will be ready to narrow down the list of colleges with excellent fit and determine if you'd like to ask for additional funds from them. For now, the focus is on submitting the financial aid applications and college applications by the deadline.

So let's take a closer look at sources of financial aid.

Sources of Aid

Money to finance a college education can come from the following sources:
1. *The federal government.* To access these funds, you must complete the FAFSA.
2. *The state government.* Some states use the FAFSA application to provide this money. Other states require students to complete a state application to access this money.
3. *The college.* Often colleges use the FAFSA to award this money. However, some colleges require students to complete the CSS Profile to access these funds.
4. *External scholarships and grants* are provided by external entities. Each scholarship or grant has its application form.

Here is a brief overview of the type of funds that are available for students filing these applications:
- FAFSA
  - Federal aid – federal grants, scholarships, loans, and work-study
  - State aid – grants and/or scholarships
  - Institutional aid – provided by some colleges, typically the funds are grants, scholarships, campus employment, or tuition waivers.
- CSS Profile

- o Institutional aid – provided by some colleges, typically the funds are grants, scholarships, campus employment, or tuition waivers.

- State Applications
  - o State aid – typically, the funds are in the form of grants or scholarships.

A college's website is the best place to learn what applications to submit in order to access this money. As you are going through the application process, you may need to fill out at least one and up to three types of financial aid forms, depending on the college and your state of residence. Therefore, it is best to plan to fill out the FAFSA and check whether colleges in your list require the completion of the CSS Profile and state applications.

Deadlines

Now that we know the type of applications and the pots of money you can access, let's talk about deadlines.

Future students are best served if they plan to submit the FAFSA and CSS Profile as soon as possible after October 1 of the fall of their senior year. For example, if your teen is planning on attending college in the fall of 2022 or during the academic year of 2022-2023 (July 1 – June 30), complete and submit the FAFSA as soon as possible after October 1, 2021. Both the FAFSA and CSS Profile open on October 1. Then double-check the state deadlines for state aid applications, and make sure you meet them.

FAFSA deadlines. One thing to note about the FAFSA is that it may have a college, state, and federal deadline. The college deadline tends to be the first one. Make sure you check the admissions website to identify the college's deadline for submitting this form.

CSS Profile Deadlines. While the CSS Profile opens on the same day as FAFSA, its submission deadlines vary by college. Go back to the college website and identify the deadlines. Remember, some colleges require that it be submitted two weeks before the deadline for the actual college application.

State Application Deadlines. Some states require residents to submit specific applications to get considered for state grants and scholarships. Florida is one of these states, and it requires residents to submit a Florida Financial Aid Application for some of its scholarships, including Bright Futures. To learn more about whether your state requires such an application check the college website or google state scholarships and grants and look at the conditions for accessing these funds. Again, not all states require these applications, but if your state does require them, make sure you add the deadlines to your list of colleges.

***

Deadlines for the college application and the financial aid application are some of the most critical deadlines you'll be working with. Having everything in one place will help ensure that you submit everything on time.

Now let's get familiar with the requirements associated with every financial aid application – FAFSA, CSS Profile, and state application.

The FAFSA Application

The Free Application for Federal Student Aid (FAFSA) is the official application that should be filed by all students seeking help to finance their college education. The FAFSA helps colleges determine how much financial assistance a student may qualify for. Students filing the FAFSA are considered for grants, scholarships, loans, work-study, or campus employment funds.

Filing the FAFSA is free, and there is no need to pay anyone to prepare it for you. In 2019, the federal government processed more than 18 million FAFSA applications. As a result, it provided more than $121 billion in aid to more than 10 million students (p. 11).[63] Almost all students who apply qualify for some federal assistance.

The FAFSA application opens on October 1 of every year. It is best to complete and file it as soon as it becomes available.

The FAFSA provides the Student Aid Index (SAI), a value formerly known as the Estimated Family Contribution (EFC). Financial aid officers use it to build the financial assistance packet.

The Student Aid Index (SAI), formerly known as the Estimated Family Contribution (EFC)
Effective October 1, 2022, the SAI replaces the EFC. Hence, anyone filing the FASFA on or after this date will receive an SAI value.

The SAI is "calculated according to a formula established by law," using FAFSA information.[64] The SAI is "an index that reflects an evaluation of a student's approximate financial resources to contribute" annually toward their education. The EFC was "defined as a measure of how much the student and his or her family can be expected to contribute to the cost" of their education annually.[65]

The change from EFC to SAI emphasizes that the SAI is a number, not the amount required to pay for college. Additionally, while the lowest EFC was zero, the SAI allows for negative values, "making it easier for colleges to identify students with the most financial need." [66] Finally, while the SAI does not vary by college, the amount of aid your teen may qualify for varies due to differences in the cost of attendance.

Federal Financial Aid Eligibility

Before going through the steps associated with filling up the FAFSA, let's see who is eligible to receive federal funds. Typically, "most U.S. citizens or eligible noncitizens" planning to attend college or a career school qualify for these funds.[67] To learn more about financial aid eligibility, go to: https://studentaid.gov/understand-aid/eligibility.
Additionally, "there is no income cut-off to qualify for federal student aid."[68]

Dependent vs. Independent Students

Now, let's take a moment to focus on the distinction between dependent and independent students. This distinction will come in handy as you prepare the documentation for FAFSA.

An independent student is "at least 24 years old, married, a graduate or professional student, a veteran, a member of the armed forces, an orphan, a ward of the court, or someone with legal dependents other than a spouse, an emancipated minor or someone who is homeless or at risk of becoming homeless."[69] A dependent student is a student who "does not meet any of the criteria for an independent student."[70] If in doubt, the federal government provides a questionnaire to help determine the dependency status: https://studentaid.gov/resources/dependency-status-text.

While the dependency rules and policies are pretty stringent, financial aid officers have the authority to change a student's dependency status under exceptional circumstances. The decision to override the federal dependency determination is granted on a case-by-case basis. Dependency overrides work in "one direction, from dependent to independent."[71] Students will need to work closely with the financial aid office to gain consideration for these overrides. To learn more about dependency overrides, go to: https://finaid.org/educators/pj/dependencyoverrides/

For the purpose of this book, the focus is on dependent students unless noted otherwise.

Test-driving the FAFSA

Suppose you are undecided about whether you should file the FAFSA and would like to review the FAFSA questions before you jump in. Or, maybe you would like to get an idea of the amount of federal aid your student may be eligible for.

The Federal Student Aid Estimator allows you to go through the FAFSA application. Once you provide the information, you'll be able to learn the amount of federal aid your student may be eligible for. The results include only the federal aid amount and exclude the state and college aid. This does not mean that your teen will not receive state and college funds; it only means that the information provided through the Estimator is related to federal funds. The Estimator is also a great way to get to an estimated SAI value. Here is the link to the Federal Student Aid Estimator: https://studentaid.gov/aid-estimator/

FAFSA & Limited Funds

Please consider submitting the FAFSA as soon as possible. The main reason for this is that financial aid funds are limited. In addition, while the federal funds your teen may qualify for are likely to remain the same independent of when you apply for them, the state and institutional funds may be awarded on a first-come-first-served basis. Therefore, the earlier you apply for aid, the better your chances of securing more financial assistance.

Put differently, the financial aid packet of two identical students is likely to look different based on the timing of the FAFSA. For example, the student who files the FAFSA earliest may get a better financial aid offer than the one who applies later.

So here is how to go about the FAFSA application.

The FAFSA Code

Each college has a unique identifier or FAFSA code. You will need this code to submit the FAFSA. There are two ways to get the college code:
1. Google the name of the college and "FAFSA code," and you should get a six-digit unique identifier, or
2. Open your list of colleges. Then look at the OPE ID column; the first six digits indicate the FAFSA code in the OPE ID column. So, you'll need to remove the last two zeroes (00) that appear at the end of the OPE ID value.

How to File the FAFSA

There are a few ways to file the FAFSA.
  a. The FAFSA app
  b. The FAFSA Website
  c. Paper

  a. The FAFSA App

This is one of the most convenient methods to file the FAFSA. It allows parents and students to collaborate and access the application from multiple devices. Also, it allows for the use of the IRS Data Retrieval Tool (IRS DRT). The FAFSA App requires FSA IDs – one for the parent and one for the student. Plan to apply for them before using the app. More details on the FSA ID and IRS DRT are included in the next section.

To download the app go to the App Store (iOS) or on Google Play (Android) and look for
 "**MyStudentAidApp**" and select the one associated with the U.S. Department of Education.[72]

b. The FAFSA website

This one is pretty straightforward. To start the FAFSA application, go to: https://studentaid.gov/h/apply-for-aid/fafsa. Here are a couple of benefits to using the online version. First, it has skip-logic technology – you'll only need to answer the questions that apply to you. Second, you'll be able to check its status and whether the completed form went through instantly using the FSA ID.[73]

c. Paper

While this is a viable option, the time needed for the colleges to get this information is extensive. Therefore, if this is the best option for you, plan to fill out the FAFSA as soon as possible after October 1, and mail it to arrive at the college on time for the financial aid officers to process it.

The FAFSA application has more than 100 questions and can be confusing. However, the form is very well put together and has skip-logic guidance, pointing students and parents to specific sections that need to be completed. Here is the link to the FAFSA application in pdf format for the 2022-2023 academic year:
 https://studentaid.gov/sites/default/files/2022-23-fafsa.pdf.

***

Once you decide on the format (app, website, or paper), you'll need to fill in the information and submit it. Keep in mind that a student will need to fill out the FAFSA every year as long as they are in college.

The U.S. Department of Education noted that it takes parents and students about one hour to fill out the FAFSA, and independent students need even less time.[74] Plus, as your student advances through college, the amount of time necessary to re-file the FAFSA decreases dramatically. This is because the App or website options tend to be less time-consuming starting with the second year, as a large portion of the form is likely to remain the same. Additionally, FAFSAs submitted using these formats are easier to revise than the paper version.

The FAFSA Application Steps

Step 1. *Apply for the FSA ID*

The first thing you'll want to do to start the FAFSA process is to apply for the Federal Student Aid Identification (FSA ID). The FSA ID is tied to the Social Security Number (SSN), and it is a unique username and password that serves as an electronic signature. The "FSA ID allows students and parents to identify themselves electronically to access Federal Student Aid websites." [75]

If you plan on filing the FAFSA online, you will need the FSA ID to sign and submit it. If your teen is a dependent student, the student and the parent will need separate FSA IDs. However, as a parent, you may already have an FSA ID from when you were a student.

To create an FSA ID, visit https://studentaid.gov/fsa-id/create-account/launch. You will need the SSN and a phone number or email address to set it up. Please note that students cannot create an FSA ID on behalf of their parents and vice-versa.

Setting up the FSA ID may take a little bit of time, and it may take a couple of days to activate. After the FSA IDs are active, you can fill out the FAFSA.

Here is guidance on the parent information that should be reported on the FAFSA: https://studentaid.gov/apply-for-aid/fafsa/filling-out/parent-info.

As the FAFSA needs to be refiled every year for college duration, you will use the FSA IDs for the subsequent annual filings.

While you can submit the FAFSA without the FSA ID, using it provides "the fastest way to sign your application and have it processed." Plus, only by using the FSA ID will you be able to "access or correct your information online, or to prefill an online FAFSA form with information from your previous year's FAFSA form." [76]

Step 2: The IRS Data Retrieval Tool

The IRS Data Retrieval Tool (IRS DRT) allows tax information to be automatically transferred into the FAFSA form. This is a great time saver, as you won't have to go around looking for the tax information. Plus, it ensures accuracy and prevents typos. While using the IRS DRT is optional, and you can enter this information manually, the burden of proof if you are selected for verification is lessened when you use it. This way, you won't need to provide additional documentation to the financial aid office.[77] About a third of the students are randomly selected for verification every year.[78]

If you file the FAFSA online, you will access the IRS DRT option. To find this option start the FAFSA application and then click on "**Link to IRS**." You'll be transferred to the IRS website. Once all the IRS information is transferred, you will be sent back to the FAFSA application. Therefore, whatever was reported to the IRS for the specified tax year will automatically populate the FAFSA form.

Plan to use the IRS DRT, especially if you filed your taxes online for the prior-prior tax year (i.e., two years ago) and are filing the FAFSA online or through the website or mobile app. If you filed the taxes by mail, you would need to allow for more than eight (8) weeks to use the IRS DRT option. Additionally, not everyone is eligible to use the IRS DRT; to learn more, go to
https://studentaid.gov/help/irs-drt-eligibility.

Again, using the IRS DRT is optional, and you can always enter this information manually. For more information on the IRS DRT, go to:
https://studentaid.gov/apply-for-aid/fafsa/filling-out.

The Work-Study on the FAFSA Form

As you are getting ready to complete and submit the FAFSA, make sure you check the Work-Study box. Work-Study funds are a special category of funds provided by the federal government directly to colleges. While not all colleges participate in the Work-Study program, those that do allow the students to earn additional income while in college. This income can be used to pay for college and decrease overall college costs.[79]

To be eligible for Work-Study funds, students need to demonstrate financial need. Financial aid officers will determine the student eligibility for these funds based on the FAFSA information.

Work-Study funds need to be earned. A student deemed eligible does not automatically get the funds but needs to find a job and earn these funds. If students are unable to find a job, they cannot earn these funds. Finding a job is not as daunting as it sounds, as many colleges have specific jobs earmarked for these students. All in all, as you are getting ready to submit your FAFSA application, the most important thing you need to know for now is to check the Work-Study box.

While federal funds such as grants and loans are unlikely to vary by the time you apply for financial aid, the Work-Study funds provided by the feds are limited. Therefore, a student who submits the FAFSA as soon as possible and is deemed eligible for work-study funds is more likely to receive them than a student who submits the FAFSA later on.[80]

Step 3: Submit the FAFSA

Once you submit the FAFSA, the Office of Federal Student Aid and the colleges you listed in the application will be notified and will be able to begin the process of building the financial aid packages.

Step 4: The SAR and the SAI

A few days after submitting the FAFSA, you will be notified of the Student Aid Report (SAR).[81] If you provided an email address on your FAFSA, "you will receive an email from *noreply@FAFSA.gov* with instructions on how to access" your online SAR.[82] Otherwise, you will receive a "SAR or a SAR Acknowledgement" through postal mail within about three weeks.[83]

Once the FAFSA information is processed, use your FSA ID to log in at fafsa.gov and access the SAR. If there are no outstanding issues with the FAFSA submission, the SAR will include the Student Aid Index (SAI). If the FAFSA is incomplete, the SAR will not include the SAI and will point to the issues that need to be addressed. The SAR "might also contain a note indicating that you've been selected for verification." [84]

The SAR summarizes the information submitted through the FAFSA. Double-check the SAR to make sure that all the information that was provided is correct.[85] One neat thing about the FAFSA is that it can be updated after it's been submitted.

Number of Colleges

The FAFSA form allows for submission to 10 colleges. However, if your teen plans to apply to more than ten colleges, the federal government provides options to deal with that. Here's how to do it: after submitting the FAFSA, you will need to "**Make a FAFSA correction**" after logging in. First, remove some colleges from your list and add the new ones. This does not mean that the colleges that you removed will not consider your teen anymore. It simply means that the colleges you removed already received your Student Aid Report (SAR), and the ones you add will also receive it.

All in all, your teen will still be considered by both sets of colleges and, if accepted, should receive financial aid letters from all the colleges. So, for example, if your teen applied to 14 colleges and was accepted by 13, within a few weeks after the acceptance letter, your teen will receive a financial aid letter from all 13 colleges. For more details, go to: <https://studentaid.gov/help/more-ten-colleges>.

While application fees can add up, applying to more than ten colleges is not uncommon. Many colleges waived the application fees during the last few admission cycles. This, combined with the ease of submitting multiple applications through platforms, such as CommonApp, led to many students applying to as many as 25 colleges and some getting admitted to 10 or more.

***

Again, submitting the FASFA is not required. However, it is wise to submit it as many federal, state, and institutional funds are awarded based on this information. You usually don't know what you may get until the financial aid letter arrives. As an admission officer explained, the worst-case scenario is that your student gets eligible only for federal loans. The best-case scenario is that your student gets surprised by the amount of aid they may receive. Hence, even under the worst-case scenario, you cannot lose. It should be noted that federal loans your teen may qualify for can be declined – meaning that if you don't want them, you don't need to accept them. However, if your student does need them, federal loans have the best rates and repayment options.

Overall, the FAFSA can help your teen qualify for thousands of dollars in aid from federal, state, or college sources, and it does not cost anything to fill out. So it may be well worth investing the time.

For FAFSA and federal aid questions visit the Federal Student Aid Information Center at https://studentaid.gov/help-center/contact.

The CSS Profile

First things first: the College Scholarship Service Profile (CSS Profile) is only required by 400 colleges. Check if any of the colleges on your list require the completion of the CSS Profile. If any college in your list requires it, read on. Otherwise, skip to the state financial aid applications section. Here is the link to the list of schools that require the CSS Profile: https://profile.collegeboard.org/profile/ppi/participatingInstitutions.aspx.

The College Board administers the College Scholarship Service Profile (CSS Profile). Unlike the FAFSA, which is free to file, the CSS Profile requires that students pay $25 to submit their information to the first college and $16 for every other college. Waivers are provided under certain circumstances. Private and public colleges and some scholarships require the completion of the CSS Profile.

Its primary purpose is to help students qualify for institutional aid. Institutional aid includes grants, scholarships, campus employment, and/or tuition waivers. It is sourced from college reserves, budgets, endowments, and/or philanthropic funds. This is typically the pot of money that admission officers can use to recruit students. Institutional aid can be allocated towards merit (scholarships), need (grants), or a combination of merit and need aid.

It is worth mentioning that students are not required to file the FAFSA or the CSS Profile. However, students can access federal aid and sometimes state and institutional assistance only if they file the FAFSA. The CSS Profile is not required either, but students seeking institutional aid (need and/or merit) should file it. If money is not an issue, there is no need to file either one of these financial aid applications.

The CSS Profile is used by colleges in addition to the FAFSA and not as a replacement for it. Colleges use the CSS Profile because it provides them with more flexibility and the ability to ask more targeted questions to evaluate the financial situation of students and their families. For example, colleges can require lots of information related to income, assets, expenses, home value, medical and childcare expenses, and so on. Financial aid officers use this information to determine a student's ability to pay for college. Depending on this, the colleges provide institutional aid to lessen the burden of college costs to future students.

The CSS Profile also provides an Estimated Family Contribution (EFC) value. However, this EFC may differ significantly from the FAFSA SAI. This is mainly because the two applications ask different questions. Additionally, each college requiring the CSS Profile uses a different formula for determining student needs and will come up with its EFC.[86] Therefore, award letters can vary significantly from college to college, even if two colleges received the same FAFSA and CSS Profile.

While the CSS Profile opens on October 1 of the fall of the senior year in high school, the deadline for submitting it varies by college. Remember, it is quite common for colleges to require that it be submitted at least two weeks before the deadline for the college application. Many colleges that use it may use Early Decision or Early Action applications. Again, make sure to keep track of all the deadlines for the college applications and the financial aid applications.

Test-driving the CSS Profile

You can test drive the CSS Profile and get an idea of your EFC. The results are estimates. Here is the link to it: https://bigfuture.collegeboard.org/pay-for-college/paying-your-share/expected-family-contribution-calculator

Documents for the CSS Profile

According to College Board, anyone preparing the CSS Profile will need their "most recently completed tax returns, W-2 forms and other records of current year income, records of untaxed income and benefits, assets and bank statements." [87] Additionally, you may need information on home equity, retirement value, childcare, eldercare, medical expenses, investments, business, farm equity, and so on.

Many colleges using the CSS Profile require financial information from both parents, even if they may be

divorced. Check with the college to determine if it requires the noncustodial parent to submit a supplemental application. Some colleges may require income information for the stepparents as well. For more information, please visit:
https://cssprofile.collegeboard.org/info-divorced-separated-parents.

Again, each college adds questions to the form, and each unique question may have a different meaning at each college. Therefore, if you need help filling it out, it is best to contact the college with your questions.

While the FAFSA should be filled out every year while a student is enrolled in college, the CSS Profile filing requirements differ by college. For example, some colleges require the CSS Profile to be submitted only for the first year, while others require it annually. Therefore, check with your college as to the frequency of completing and submitting it.

Unlike the FAFSA, the CSS Profile allows students and parents to provide additional details and context to the financial information.

The CSS Profile cannot be revised after submitting it. Therefore, if you discover any typos or errors after submitting it, the corrections will need to be sent to each college in writing.

If you submit the FAFSA and the CSS Profile, colleges will use information from both to allocate federal and institutional aid. Therefore, make sure that the two forms are in sync.

As you've probably guessed by now, completing the CSS Profile tends to require significantly more time than FAFSA.

State Financial Aid Applications

Some states have specific forms that students can use to apply for state aid. These state forms are in addition to the FAFSA and the CSS Profile. Check out the college website or talk to your high school counselor to determine what documents you need to complete in addition to FAFSA to qualify for state aid. For example, Florida requires students to file separate applications for state scholarships and grants.[88] This application has its own deadlines.

Some states require that these applications be re-filed each year a student is enrolled in college. Double-check to see if these applications need to be re-filled annually.

Keeping Track of Everything

Phew, we are almost there. So now that you know what's next in terms of financial aid applications, make sure to pay attention to the deadlines.

If you are like me and like to see/feel the documents, rather than have them in some emails somewhere, set up a folder with FAFSA and other financial aid application documents. You may want to set up the file folder during the summer before senior year of high school and add documents to it as your teen advances through the college application process. Also, this folder will come in handy, as FAFSA needs to be re-filed every year as long as a student is enrolled in college. This way, you'll be able to file the FAFSA every year as soon as it opens on October 1.

Here is a list of documents that you may need to file the FAFSA, CSS Profile, and/or state applications. Dependent students will need this information for themselves and their parents:

- The Social Security Number
- The Alien Registration Number, for non-U.S. citizens
- The federal income tax returns, W-2s, and other records of money earned.
- Bank statements and records of investments
- Records of untaxed income
- The FSA IDs[89] and login information for the CSS Profile and state applications
- Anything else you deem appropriate to help with the financial aid applications.

***

Remember, the FAFSA can be revised after submission, but the CSS Profile cannot. Plus, submitting the FAFSA and state applications is free, but there is a fee associated with submitting the CSS Profile.

Here are a few important reminders about applying for financial aid
1. FAFSA
    o Filing the FAFSA is free. File it even if you think you don't qualify for any aid.
    o Most colleges use FAFSA to award federal, state, and institutional aid.
    o Pay close attention to the year when your teen will enroll in college and file the FAFSA application for that year.

- Pay close attention to the FAFSA deadlines and plan to submit it as soon as possible after October 1 of every year.
- The best way to file it is online (app or website).
- It needs to be re-filed for each year the student enrolls in college. Using one of these options will save time with re-filing it.

2. CSS Profile
    - About 400 colleges across the U.S. require it and there is a fee associated with submitting it.
    - Check college websites to figure out which colleges require it.
    - Submit everything by the deadlines.

3. State Applications
    - Some states require students to submit separate applications for state grants and scholarships in addition to the FAFSA.
    - Check state and college websites to determine which states require it.
    - Submit everything by the deadline.

The DSSL Excel File

If you haven't had a chance to add the extra columns to your Starter List, you can still download Diana's Sample Starter List (DSSL) and copy the columns.

The DSSL file includes all the columns provided by the College Navigator through the "Export Results" option, plus all the additional columns that we'll add in the previous chapters. Specifically, you will get a file with about 16 columns through the College Navigator "Export." Then you'll have to add about 12 more to it.

The DSSL file includes all these 28 columns plus three colleges as a sample. Scan the QR code included below to download the DSSL file. You can copy and paste all the 12 column headings from the DSSL file and add them to your Starter List that you'll download from College Navigator.

Summary

Great job! You just finished the second most challenging step in the college admission process. Kudos to you! Everything becomes more manageable now.

Now your most important task is to wait for the colleges' decision patiently, well, as patiently and calmly as you can. I am still trying to get better at learning patience every day.

As admission decisions are coming in, the next step is to weigh each one of them carefully. The next part discusses different types of admission decisions, explains each one of them, and provides guidance on how to address them.

Part IV
ADMISSION DECISIONS

Chapter 13: Types of Decisions and Next Steps

So here we are, your teen submitted applications to all the colleges on their list, and now we wait for the admission decisions. This chapter walks you through the types of admission decisions, what they mean, and how to use them to your advantage.

Here are the most common admission decisions your teen may receive:
- Accepted
- Conditional acceptance
- Accepted for another term
- Waitlisted
- Deferred
- Rejected

Let's discuss each one of these options.

Accepted

Congratulations! Your teen is in.

This calls for a celebration — pat yourselves on the back. You did great and got in. But decision time, i.e., the time to decide which college to attend, has not come yet.

The college has accepted your teen, and the path now is very straightforward. This may be the time when you learn about some gift aid, especially merit aid. Some colleges will use the acceptance letter or notification to let you know how much gift aid your teen qualifies for if they enroll. Others will send you the acceptance letter and guide you on the next steps.

Next, you'll wait some more. The next document or notification you'll get is the financial aid award offer. You will receive financial aid letters (FAL) or "award letters" after receiving the acceptance letters. Each college that admits your teen will provide you with one. Some colleges offer FALs within a few days after the acceptance letters, while others provide them within a few weeks. However, this is a time of waiting, waiting for more admission decisions and financial aid offers. This is the time to focus 100% on senior year activities - study, pictures, prom, friendships, and so on.

While you wait, order the next book in this series. That book will help you:
- Understand the meaning of the elements included in the financial aid offer
- Learn how to determine your out-of-pocket costs for each college
- Compare colleges on out-of-pocket costs

- Determine your financial fit
- Learn how to go about asking the colleges for more aid

All in all, *The Ultimate College Financial Aid Guide: Understand the Aid Offer & Ask for More Money* book will help you ascertain the last element of fit - financial fit.

Remember, students who apply using early decision (ED) commit to attending a college at the time of application. Therefore, if the college admits them, they'll get only one financial aid letter – hence they will not know how much aid another college might offer. In other words, ED applicants determine most of their financial fit at the time of application.

"Accepted" is an outcome that everyone strives for. However, it should be noted that not everyone who is not accepted is rejected. Therefore, let's explore the other possible admission outcomes.

Conditional Acceptance

Conditional acceptance is another important admission outcome. It can mean different things at different colleges, but it generally refers to the fact that a student must do something before gaining full admission at the C/U. Here are some scenarios for conditional acceptance.

First, conditionally admitted students need to meet specific requirements to be fully accepted by the college. For example, some colleges require students to take certain classes at the local community college and secure a certain GPA. Then if the student crosses the GPA threshold, the student will be fully admitted to the C/U.

Other colleges require conditional admit students to enroll in the online branch or at a branch campus (not the main one) of the college. Again, this is quite common, especially for large colleges. Under this scenario, students may need to take a few or the majority of their freshman or sophomore classes online or at the branch campus. Also, some colleges require their conditional admit students to live on campus, even if they can only take online courses.

All in all, each college handles conditional acceptances differently. Therefore, the best way to learn what conditional admission means for a college is through the admission letter and the college's website.

This begs the question of should your teen attend if they are a conditional admit? Well, there is no right or wrong answer to this. However, the issue of fit and other acceptances should help guide this decision. Therefore, think critically about all the fit dimensions – academic, personal, and financial in the context of other admission and financial aid offers – and decide accordingly.

Accepted for a Different Term

Another way to get accepted by a college is to get accepted for a different term. In other words, your teen may have applied for next fall. However, colleges can accept students for a term different than next fall. That term can be the summer or the following spring.

Summer

Students who apply for the fall semester may get accepted for the summer semester instead. Some colleges identify students who may be a great fit and may need a little bit of help to get up to speed. These students may get admitted to the summer term. This ensures that students get up to speed with college processes and transition smoothly into the fall semester. If your teen has been admitted for the summer term, they'll probably need to be on campus earlier than other students and will need to participate in certain activities. This is a great way to understand the college's mechanics, ease into college, and take advantage of everything it has to offer.

Spring

I've seen spring admissions gain popularity during the last several years. This is a way for colleges to mitigate against student loss from fall because some students who enroll in the fall semester may not return for the spring semester. Plus, students at all levels graduate on an ongoing basis. Therefore, accepting and enrolling students for the spring semester can be a way for colleges to maintain their enrollment levels.

If the college accepts your teen for the spring semester, you may have to make a few decisions. First, you need to decide if you want to attend that college – again, evaluate fit.

If students decide to commit to a college and start in spring, they have a few options. They may choose to take a break, relax, volunteer, look for a job, or even travel abroad.

Second, they may want to consider taking classes at the local community college and transferring those courses to the college later. A point of clarification is needed here. The local community college is actually the community college closest to the C/U they'll be attending in the spring. If the college your teen plans to attend is out of state, however, and your teen wants to take classes at your neighboring community college, then you'll need to transfer those credits across state lines. The chances of the C/U accepting credits from an out-of-state community college tend to be relatively low, unfortunately. More about credit transfer in Chapter 17.

Also, keep in mind that starting in the spring may delay your teen's college graduation. However, they may be able to mitigate that by enrolling for a higher course load at a later point. Part V discusses on-time graduation and how to graduate college with the least amount of debt.

Waitlisted

Being waitlisted is an important admission decision that requires serious consideration on the part of the student.

Students who are waitlisted are, in essence, neither accepted nor rejected. Specifically, they are in a holding space where they need to decide how they'd like to proceed forward. An admission officer compared the waitlist with "the seventh layer of the admissions purgatory." [90]

A waitlist acts as a buffer for the college. In essence, the college admits a number of students and adds some to the waitlist. Therefore, if too many admitted students decide to enroll somewhere else, the college will pull some students from the waitlist and admit them. The waitlist allows a college to meet its priorities and goals.[91] Remember Universal Truth #3 – *it's not about you*; the college admission decision is always about the college and its priorities.

A 2019 report found that colleges with lower selectivity and yield "were more likely to use waitlists." [92] Colleges use waitlists for a variety of reasons. One is the concern over yield or how many students eventually enroll at the college.

Let's start at the beginning. Colleges have a certain number of spots to fill for their fall class. Therefore, they admit a certain percentage of students out of all the applicants, hence the selectivity metric. But only a portion of the students they admit will enroll at the college; this is the yield metric.

Many colleges becoming test-optional has led to a significant increase in applicants.[93] During the Fall of 2021 admission cycle, many students applied to as many as 20 colleges. It does not matter how many of these colleges accepted them because one student can only attend one college.

Admission officers know this. And selectivity and yield are both essential for students, parents, and colleges. Therefore, admission officers carefully assess college applications to identify who would actually enroll at the college if admitted.

To ensure that the college fills up its class, colleges admit students knowing that only a certain percentage of them will enroll. Then they add a significant number of students to the waitlist, just in case more students than expected decide to enroll somewhere else.

Colleges usually aim for low selectivity rate and high yield rate. Hence, colleges want a high percentage of the students admitted to enroll. The Harvards and Stanfords of the world illustrate these metrics best. They have a selectivity rate of about 5% (meaning they are highly selective: they only accept 5% of their applicant) and a yield rate of about 70%. All colleges aspire to values like these, but few achieve them. Waitlisting is a way to increase yield without increasing selectivity rate too much because students who end up on the waitlist usually have to re-iterate their commitment to attend if accepted. So admission officers know that the students who end up being admitted from the waitlist will attend.

Here is what this looks like in practice. Let's say College A wants to enroll 300 new students next fall. Let's say that the college's selectivity is 50% and the yield is 30%.

For a class of 300, the college will need to have 2,000 applicants. Accept 1,000 of them (50% selectivity). Then be sure that 300 (30% yield) of them will enroll at the college next fall.

But to be even safer, the college puts about 300 to 400 on the waitlist from the 1,000 applicants who were not accepted.

In essence, the college is hedging its bets. For example, if more students than expected enrolled at other colleges (i.e., their yield is in danger of decreasing), then the college can add students from the waitlist to the fall class.

For example, in the Fall of 2017 Brown University class was 1,719 students, but for the fall of 2018, they admitted 2,566 and waitlisted 2,724 students. In essence, "if every single admitted applicant rejected Brown's offer, it would have waitlist candidates to spare in building a class larger than the last one." Likewise, the University of Pennsylvania admitted "3,731 applicants for the next first-year class, anticipated to be 2,445 students" and waitlisted around 3,500 students.[94] Examples like these abound.

Additionally, admission officers note that "being on the waitlist is not a ticket to getting in," [95] and waitlisted students are unlikely to get admitted[96]. For example, UPenn accepted between 20 and 175 students from its waitlist.[97] Another college noted that the "number of students who are eventually offered a spot is unpredictable, and has varied in recent years from as few as 12 to more than 50." [98] Additionally, the NACAC 2019 report noted that "selective colleges were least likely to admit students from a waitlist."[99]

Colleges are also using waitlists to avoid rejecting students. Colleges do not want to "offend alumni when they reject their children" [100] and "want to be respectful of how hard they've worked and how difficult it is to receive an outright rejection." [101]

So now that you know the mechanics behind it, here's how to proceed if your teen ends up on a waitlist.

First, the college may provide you with specific instructions on the next steps. Many will ask if you'd like to retain a spot on the waitlist. You may need to complete a form for that.

Second, follow the steps required by the college. One admission officer noted that students should try to "not stalk the admissions office." [102]

Third, keep an open mind and take a closer look at the colleges that accepted your teen. Evaluate them closely, and I am pretty sure you'll be able to find and appreciate some of their most attractive and enticing features.

Moreover, remember Universal Truth #4 – *you have options*. This may be the perfect time to pull out your balanced list of colleges from your back-pocket and maybe consider submitting a few more applications.[103]

Additionally, make sure your teen commits to a college before May 1st (College Decision Day). It is best to play it safe and have a clear plan for the fall. If colleges that waitlisted them come back after this date, they'll decide what to do then.

Finally, the best thing you could do now is to help your teen focus on their high school studies. Make sure they do their best academically and enjoy all the senior year activities such as prom, friendships, activities, and so on.[104]

Remember, not all colleges use waitlists. Some disclose the number of students who end up on waitlists through the Common Data Set (CDS). If you are interested in seeing whether any of your colleges use waitlists, google the college's name and CDS. The waitlist information is included in section C. Again, not all colleges fill out the CDS, publish it, or answer all questions. You may find colleges that publish the number of students waitlisted and the number of students admitted from the waitlist. But some colleges may or may not provide these values.

While I do not have experience with the waitlists, I do have plenty of experiences with being in limbo while waiting for a decision. For example, I remember the beginning of my junior year in college. This was when students learned if they'd get merit aid for the term. And boy, did I need the money! I started working that fall because I needed the money to help my mom with various expenses.

So here I was at the beginning of my junior year, the scholarship committee was deciding which GPA would be the cutoff. I was right on the cusp. The registrar's office posted a list of students, and I was the last one on the list. So one day, I'd walk by and read the list, and I'd be on it. The next day I'd walk by and read the list, and I would be off it, and so on. This lasted for about two weeks. Well, I did not get merit aid for that term, but the sleepless nights and the anxiety were just so overwhelming. I eventually did get the scholarship the following term and for the remainder of college. But I learned that uncertainty and limbo are part of the process.

All in all, if your teen ends up on a waitlist, help them identify what they really want. Take some time to reassess the other acceptance offers. Help them identify a college with a great fit and commit to it by the May 1st deadline. Then, if the college that waitlisted your teen comes through, they'll decide if they'd still like to attend it. And try not to lose sleep over it. Remember, admission decisions rely heavily on college's priorities, goals, and factors outside of your control.

Deferred

Deferred students are in a slightly different position than the waitlisted ones. All in all, "being deferred means you have more waiting to do." [105]

This is where the meaning of deferred starts to vary by college. At some colleges, being deferred means "*hold on, we're not sure, we'd like to see more.*" [106, 107] While at other colleges, being deferred means "*we need more time.*" [108]

Students who applied Early Action (EA) or Early Decision (ED) and have been deferred may have their applications automatically moved into the Regular Decision pool of applicants. The deferral is significant, especially if your teen applied ED. The deferred decision releases students from the binding contract.[109] In other words, if an ED college deferred your teen but accepts them during Regular Decision, your teen is no longer required to attend that college.

If your teen has been deferred, the college may ask for additional documents. Some of these documents may include senior year grades, maybe additional test scores, [110] an additional essay, or perhaps an interview. [111] An admission officer advised students to read the deferral letter carefully, follow the steps outlined, and provide only the documents required by the admission office, and nothing more.[112]

Being deferred does not mean being rejected or denied. It means that the student is competitive and maybe a good fit; otherwise, your teen would have been denied admission.[113] However, a deferred student's chances for entry are not great either.[114] Similar to being waitlisted, deferred applicants should choose a college and commit by May 1st. If the college comes back with an offer after May 1st, then you'll weigh in your options again. So, play it safe and have a clear plan for the fall.

Deferred students may want to weigh carefully the colleges that admitted them and maybe consider applying to more colleges.

Rejected

Remember Universal Truth #3 – *it's not about you*. Please repeat after me: admission decisions are college-specific, outside of your control, and are not a reflection of a student's efforts. Plus, remember that a student getting rejected by a college does not mean that another will reject them as well.

Plus, remember Universal Truth #1 – *colleges need students just as much as students need colleges*. I hope that this walkthrough of various admission decisions has solidified this understanding.

I firmly believe that students who do their best to build a balanced college list will get more admission letters rather than fewer. Therefore, if the first college students applied to rejects them, they should not take it to heart. Applying to the rest of the colleges on their balanced list and doing their best with those applications will go a long way. More often than not, the challenge you'll face will be deciding between the colleges that accepted your teen, and not the lack of acceptance letters.

Then, even if lacking acceptance letters is a problem, remember, there is always a solution and a path forward.

Applying to Rolling Admission colleges, starting at the community college, or applying for admission for the spring semester are great options. Always remember you have options.

***

The college admissions world is nuanced. As you can see, when it comes to college admissions, the opposite of acceptance is not rejection.

The next step is to wait for the financial aid offers from all the colleges that admitted your teen. Then [read the financial aid book](#) to learn how to make sense of it all and save money on college. Then identify the college with the best financial fit and weigh that information in relation to academic and personal fit.

The remainder of this book explains how to use high school work and college strategies to graduate college on time and keep college costs to a minimum. Read this part before committing to a college, as the information included here can help you save thousands of dollars.

Finally, you'll have to find the college with the best fit and highest likelihood of graduating on-time and then will have to commit to it before May 1st.

Part V
MINIMIZE COLLEGE COSTS

This is the time when you are probably awaiting the financial aid offer from various colleges. As you are getting ready to weigh them and determine financial fit, here are a few things to keep in mind that can inform the college selection and help your teen complete college almost debt-free.

As you have just completed the admission process, you may feel that college graduation at this point is a distant goal. But you'll want to read this section now to keep college costs to a minimum. Here you'll learn how to make the most out of your teen's high school work and plan the freshman year to ensure no burn-out. Plus, you can work to minimize the possibility of being blindsided by any unforeseen costs related to delays in graduation or credit transfer.

Chapter 14 provides a quick overview of the typical length of a bachelor's program and on-time graduation.

Chapter 15 explains how to use credits earned during high school to help your teen advance toward college graduation.

Chapter 16 focuses on college strategies you and your teen can use to minimize college costs and ensure on-time graduation.

Chapter 17 focuses on the transfer process. First, we discuss the benefits and challenges associated with credit transfer. Then we'll focus on strategies to help ensure a smooth and seamless transfer process that will lead to on-time college graduation.

Chapter 14: On-Time Graduation

Before we talk about how to keep college costs to a minimum, let's focus on the length of a college degree and understand the meaning of on-time graduation.

On-time graduation means that a student completes all the college courses in the appropriate sequence to graduate in 4-years. As you probably remember from the graduation rates section, the standard used for measuring college graduation is set at the 6-year mark, not the 4-year one.

Bachelor's Program Length. So let's unpack this a bit more. Most college degrees – bachelor's programs – require that students complete at least 120 credits to graduate. These credits can be split across semesters or terms. While the way the colleges measure credits may vary by college and accreditation agency, a typical college course that is assigned a 3-hour class per week for 15 weeks usually equals 3 credits for that semester. Some courses have anywhere from 1 to 4 credits associated with them.

In more technical terms, the definition of a credit hour is that for each one hour spent in class, a student should allocate two more hours for study (readings, homework, preparation for quizzes, and so on).[115] This is important from the perspective of trying to graduate on time and working while in college.

Simple math shows that if a student takes 15 credits a semester, their weekly class course load and out-of-class effort should be around 45 (=15 x 3) hours per week. As you can see, this is more than a full-time job. Therefore, if your teen plans to work while in college, make sure they strike a decent balance between work hours and college work. That will help students avoid burn-out and be on track to graduate on time.

Scholars have found that students who work more than 20 hours a week are very likely to experience delays in college graduation. In addition, delays in graduation can be very costly (Hayes, 2010). We'll touch on this shortly.

On-Time Graduation. Students are considered to be on track to graduate college in 4 years if they complete no fewer than 30 credits per academic year. An academic year usually consists of a fall, spring, and summer semester. Many colleges will tell you that a student who was a freshman in the fall of 2021 will be a sophomore in the fall of 2022 if they completed no fewer than 30 credits before fall 2022. Otherwise, the student will still be considered a freshman for college tracking purposes. In other words, the sophomore and higher levels are assigned by the number of credits completed, not by the number of years spent in college.

To add an extra layer of complexity, completing 30 credits at random – i.e., unrelated to one's major – does not necessarily mean that a student is on track to graduate on time. In other words, exploration in college is a good thing, but being smart about course selection can help a student graduate on time and almost debt-free.

Academic advisers will come in handy with course selection to ensure in-major progression. At the same time, academic advisers will also help students identify the major that would fit them best, should they come into college undecided.

All of this goes back to paying close attention to a college's student support services because they can make a huge difference for students and help minimize college costs.

Remember the graduation rates section. These rates point to on-time or delayed graduation. At the national level, about 40% of students graduate in 4 years and about 60% in 6 years.

This information may be critical when you'll need to finalize the academic, personal, and financial fit and commit to a college. As an aside, engineering programs are usually longer programs and require more credits – around 130. Therefore, students in these programs typically need five years to graduate.

Also, it should be noted that as students progress through college, things become more manageable, and they get used to the academic standards and expectations and can increase their course load. In other words, it is my recommendation that students pace themselves, especially during the freshman year, and then increase the course load as they advance through their years of study.

Therefore, use the strategies discussed in this part to learn how to help your students pace themselves through college to ensure on-time graduation.

Chapter 15: Using High School Work to Earn College Credit

You may have already heard parents boasting about how their teen started college almost as a sophomore. How they saved one or two years' worth of college costs because of the work their teen completed in high school.

This is possible using college preparatory courses that students complete in high school. These are the Advanced Placement (AP), International Baccalaureate (IB), or Dual Enrollment (DE) courses. These courses serve triple duty for high school students as they can count towards:
1. High school graduation
2. College admission
3. College credit

Advanced Placement (AP) and International Baccalaureate (IB) Courses

As you probably remember, admission officers' second most important factor when making college decisions is grades in college preparatory courses. These courses are great because, if used wisely, they may decrease college costs in two ways – by helping students earn more merit aid and getting colleges to count them towards college graduation.

Let's take a tiny step back and explain the role of AP/IB courses in the HSGPA and college credit.

Advanced Placement (AP) and International Baccalaureate (IB) courses have two components. First, a student takes the class in high school, completes the work, and gets a grade based on this work. This grade then counts towards the HSGPA. The second component relates to the exam. These courses have exams associated with them, and students get a certain score. Students pay a fee to take these exams.

Colleges use the score from this exam and award college credit depending on how high the score is. For example, some colleges may award 4 college credits for a score of 4 on the AP Chemistry exam and 8 credits for a score of 5. Assuming a hypothetical cost per college credit of $300, a college awarding 4 credits means that a student may save $1,200 in college expenses. Again, it all depends on the college and its policies.

It is not uncommon for students to earn up to 50 college credits using these courses, saving them about 1.5 years of college.

Here are a few things to consider regarding these courses and college credit. First, the courses and exams associated with these courses tend to be quite challenging. From the perspective of the HSGPA, these courses will enhance it, mainly when calculating the weighted HSGPA. In other words, getting A's in these courses is not that easy, and if the HSGPA is not weighted, these grades can bring it down. Remember weighing means that a grade of A in AP Chemistry is assigned 5 points (rather than 4 points, when the grade is un-weighted) for the HSGPA. Plus, remember that each college decides whether and how to weigh HSGPAs.

Second, colleges have different policies regarding these courses. There are two options for awarding college credits – decrease or replacement. Let's unpack this a little bit. Let's say that your teen secured a score of 5 on the AP Chemistry exam (not the high school class grade), and a college awards them 8 college credits for it.

Colleges using the "decrease" policy will subtract the number of credits required to complete the bachelor's program from the total. Specifically, for a decrease, the college decides that your teen will have to complete only 112 (= 120 - 8) credits, and hence you have, in essence, saved on tuition and other costs.

Under the "replace" policy, the fact that colleges award credit for these courses does not necessarily mean that the overall number of credits decreases. Therefore, the college may award 8 college credits, but the overall number of credits that must be completed remains the same. Your teen will still have to pay for all the 120 credit hours, except that they have now gained the flexibility to replace those 8 credits with other courses they may be interested in. Plus, your teen may be able to skip some college chemistry classes.

Third, not all colleges award credit for these courses. While many colleges consider these courses for admission, some do not award college credit for them.

***

Again, the importance of college preparatory courses cannot be understated for college admission purposes. Taking a good look at which colleges award credits and their policies around these credits will help you determine which college will help you save the most money.

Dual Enrollment (DE) Courses

Dual Enrollment (DE) is another way to earn college credit during high school. These courses are typically regular college courses that students can complete while in high school.

Some colleges offer Dual Enrollment (DE) courses at a high school, typically with instructors vetted by the college. Other times high school students enroll in DE courses offered on a college or university campus. Under this scenario, the high school student is typically in the same class as college students.

Like AP and IB, DE courses can enhance a high school student's application for college. These courses show academic rigor and that students challenged themselves and persevered. Additionally, similar to AP/IB courses, students enrolled in DE courses get a grade added to the high school transcript. However, unlike AP/IB, DE courses don't have exams associated with them.

Here are a few things to keep in mind about DE courses. First, some states offer DE courses for free to their high school students. Therefore, these courses can add up to significant savings in tuition and fees.

Second, DE courses are transferrable within the state. In other words, students who know that they would like to attend college in their home state can use DE to decrease college costs. Conversely, DE courses typically don't transfer across state lines. Therefore, high school students completing DE courses in one state may not be able to transfer them to a college outside of the state. However, each college is different, and it is always a good idea to check whether an out-of-state college will accept these credits for transfer.

Additionally, some states allow high school students to complete Associate of Arts degrees through DE courses. In essence, students can earn a high school diploma and an Associate in Arts degree upon high school graduation. Then your teen can transfer this Associate of Arts degree to a college and start college as a junior and may be able to graduate with a bachelor's degree two years later. As a result, students and parents can save significantly on college expenses. To learn if this option is available in your state, contact your high school counselor and check the transfer requirements for the college that your teen would like to attend.

While this sounds very enticing, DE courses are, in essence, college-level courses and can entail a significant amount of work. If your teen is interested in pursuing this option, make sure you have all the knowledge necessary to navigate the process.

***

Overall, college preparatory courses can bring significant college savings. The key is to understand both sides of the "equation," if you will. First, you'll need to find out which courses are available at your teen's high school and what policies are in place to allow students to enroll and complete them. Plan to contact your high school counselors to learn more about the high school policies. Second, try to get familiar with the college's policies about these courses. Visit college websites to understand how colleges treat and award credits for these courses.

Chapter 16: Using College Smarts to Graduate Almost Debt-Free

So let's explore some strategies that students can use in college to minimize college costs and ensure on-time graduation.

Summer Courses

Students can pace themselves through college and ensure a good college GPA by registering for summer courses. This is a great idea, especially during the freshman year.

First year is unique in that many high school graduates may experience the college transition shock. This occurs because many first-year students are usually not familiar with the college standards and the amount of time needed to study for college courses. This may lead to lower GPAs from the get-go. And increasing a low starting GPA requires a lot of work later on.

Researchers found that a common reason for GPA decreases is the difference between high school and college standards. College standards tend to be more stringent, and students may need a little bit of time to adjust to them. A student who used to get A's in high school may start getting other grades in college, thus influencing their GPA. A Berkeley study found that "mean [college] GPAs plummeted well below what students have become accustomed to earning in high school," noting that the mean high school GPA of 3.52 decreased to 2.97 after the first year of college (Geiser and Santelices, 2007, p. 17).

Because of the transition shock, it may be a good idea for first-year students to register for the smallest amount of credits that qualify them for the full-time load during the fall and spring semesters. This will be 12 credits (roughly four courses) per semester at many colleges. Then use the summer semester to pick 6 more credits (approximately two courses). Therefore, they'd complete 30 credit hours for the year and be on track to graduate college in 4 years. All in all, it is quite common for students to experience a decrease in GPA during first year. I have to say that I experienced this transition shock during my first year in college and master's degree. That is to say, very few people are immune to this transition.

Registering for summer classes is possible at (1) the home college/university (C/U) or (2) the local community college. First, your teen can register for summer classes at their C/U. Make sure that the courses they register for can be counted towards their major, if not as required, then as electives. My point is that when almost debt-free is the focus, students may want to minimize the number of courses that are not counting towards the major and degree.

Second, some colleges allow students to register for summer classes at their local community college and transfer the credits. This is a good option, as credits at the community college may be significantly cheaper than at the home college. Here are two things to keep in mind if your teen plans to pursue this option. First, make sure that the courses they plan to complete at the community college transfer to the home institution. Ensure that the home C/U (where your teen is pursuing their degree) will accept and count them towards the major/degree. Always check with the home institution first, and if they accept these credits, then proceed to complete them at the community college.

Plus, always check with the home institution to see whether they have a cutoff for the grades they will accept for transfer. In other words, universities may not accept courses completed with grades below a specific cutoff, i.e., B- or below. Again, all of this varies by home institution.

All in all, if planning to enroll in summer courses at the local community college, start the process at the home institution and make sure you are familiar with all the conditions associated with transferring those credits and counting them towards the college degree.

***

Remember, for students to stay on track and graduate in 4 years, they need to complete no fewer than 30 credits per year. Failure to do so will add time to their degree – making the college degree more costly.

Gift Aid Decreases

Pacing oneself through college is especially important from the gift aid perspective because a lot of gift aid is tied to the college GPA.

Gift aid, in essence, is money that does not have to be repaid, and it's in the form of grants or scholarships. Students learn about gift aid through financial aid letters.

Grant Aid. Let's break it down a little more. Grants are awarded to students based on demonstrated financial need. First, the student submits financial information through the FAFSA, CSS Profile, or other state financial aid applications. Second, the financial aid officers review this information and award aid to students.

Grants can be provided by the federal government, state, or college. Some Ivy League schools are famous for providing large grants for students who demonstrate financial need. It is essential to know that maintaining eligibility for grants is based on two factors: (1) continued demonstrated financial need and (2) satisfactory academic progress.

First, students need to refile the financial aid application every year while in college to demonstrate financial need. Changes in family finances can prompt changes in the amount of aid a student receives. For example, decreases in AGI (Adjusted Gross Income) for the student and their family (if the student is dependent for financial aid purposes) may help the student qualify for increased grants. Conversely, income increases may prevent students from qualifying for these funds.

Second, students need to meet the Satisfactory Academic Progress (SAP) requirements to continue to receive grant aid. The SAP requirements are established by each college individually. They usually entail a certain GPA and specific requirements for course progression.

Scholarship Aid. Many scholarships are typically awarded due to academic achievement. Some of these scholarships may be only a one-time award (scholarships for the first year in college) or renewable (sometimes for up to 8 semesters). One of the most important things to keep in mind about scholarships is that they have specific requirements for renewal. In general, the requirements include maintaining a certain GPA, completing service hours, volunteering, performance (for music majors), athletic performance, and so on.

Unfortunately, it is common to lose funding for college by losing eligibility for gift aid. This can present students and parents with the need to borrow to finance their education. Do your best to learn all the conditions and terms related to gift aid renewal to ensure that your teen maintains eligibility for the funds.

Pay for 15, Register for 18 or More

Some colleges let students pay a flat fee and register for many credits per semester. For example, one college may allow students who pay for 15 credits for a semester to register for 18 or more. While it is true that this is a heavy load for a semester, being able to do this will accelerate a student's studies and significantly decrease college costs.

While decreasing college costs is very important, planning for an increased load is wise starting with the second year or later. Plus, students registering for an increased load should balance work and other responsibilities wisely so as not to keep them away from their studies.

Extra Semesters in College

Extra semesters in college can lead to delays in graduation. These delays can be caused by various factors, such as working, finances, course selection, and so on. The issue is that these delays may translate into high costs for students and their families.

A 2010 study explored the financial impact of delaying college graduation by one or two years after the 4-year mark. The study used 2010 values for tuition costs, post-graduation salary, interest rates, and "the opportunity costs of professional advancement and retirement contributions." [116] It found that one extra year spent in college after the 4-year mark can cost a student anywhere between $95,000 and $115,000 in lost revenues over a lifetime. A two-year delay in graduation was found to cost between $141,000 and $186,000 (p. 10). Remember, these are 2010 values with lower tuition costs and lower expected salaries. However, these values are likely to increase when using the 2021 tuition and salary levels.

All in all, delays in graduation may increase college costs and decrease lifetime earnings. Using graduation rates during the selection process will help you identify your teen's probability of completing a college degree on-time.

Negotiate the Financial Aid Offer

The next book in this series discusses the Financial Aid offer and everything you need to know about it. It explains the meaning of each element that appears in the offer, and more importantly, it describes how to negotiate or appeal for more aid. Until you get all your financial aid offers, one of the most important things to keep in mind is that you can and should negotiate your financial aid offer.

***

In conclusion, pacing oneself through college is essential. Using advisers to pick and choose the right courses to keep a student on track for on-time graduation can play a significant role in lifetime earnings. Additionally, being smart about the number of hours worked during college can enhance a student's earnings.

Chapter 17: The Transfer Option

Transfer is a natural part of the college experience; about 35% of students attend more than one university or college during their college careers (Simone 2014).

Transfer can take many flavors. It can include transfer from a community college to a university, between universities, and even from a university to a community college. However, the purpose is to carry the credit for learning already completed to another institution and apply it towards earning a bachelor's degree. Here are the three common types of transfer:

(1) **Vertical transfer** occurs when a student transfers from a 2-year institution (typically a community college) to a 4-year institution (typically a university or liberal arts college). This is the most common type of transfer and the most efficient one.

(2) **Horizontal transfer** occurs when a student attempts to transfer credits between two similar institutions, for example, from a community college to another community college or from a university to another university or liberal arts college.

(3) **Reverse transfer** occurs when a student attempts to transfer from a 4-year institution (typically a university or liberal arts college) to a 2- year institution (typically a community college).

Vertical Transfer

For this chapter, we'll focus on vertical transfer. This chapter provides actionable information to help you transfer the maximum number of credits from a community college to a university or liberal arts college. We'll discuss the benefits and challenges associated with college transfer and strategies to ensure a smooth transfer.

Benefits

Starting at the community college and transferring to the university to complete a college degree is quite common and provides several benefits. First, parents and students can significantly decrease college costs when this process works seamlessly. This is because the cost per credit tends to be substantially lower at community colleges than at universities most of the time. Completing about half of a bachelor's degree at a community college can bring significant savings.

Second, students can skip standardized testing requirements. Community colleges are open admission, meaning that they will accept anyone who applies. Therefore, future students can submit tests scores if they want to, but are not required to do so. In addition, most universities do not require transfer students to submit standardized scores for admission.

Third, students pursuing the vertical transfer option can earn a credential along the way. This credential – called the Associate of Arts – can play a significant role in smoothing the transfer process and preventing credit loss.

All in all, vertical transfer is efficient because it tends to keep credit loss to a minimum. Plus, vertical transfer plays an essential role in providing students access to a college degree and significant upward mobility.

Challenges

While there are significant benefits to vertical transfer, here are some challenges associated with it.

First, a significant area of focus associated with vertical transfer is the challenge of completing a bachelor's degree. A transfer research overview published in 2015 by the Community College Research Center, associated with Columbia University, noted that 80% of the students who start at a community college plan to transfer to a 4-year institution and complete a bachelor's degree. However, only 25% of these students did transfer, and out of these, only 62% graduated with a bachelor's degree 6 years later – see Figure 17.1. In other words, only 17% of the students who started at the community college with an intent to graduate with a bachelor's degree did so 6 years later.[117] In addition, credit loss during transfer was found to play an essential role in the bachelor attainment rates.[118] Therefore, the remainder of the chapter focuses on strategies to ensure a smooth transfer process and mitigate credit loss.

Figure 17.1: Percent of transfer students who started at a community college and completed a bachelor's degree 6 years later

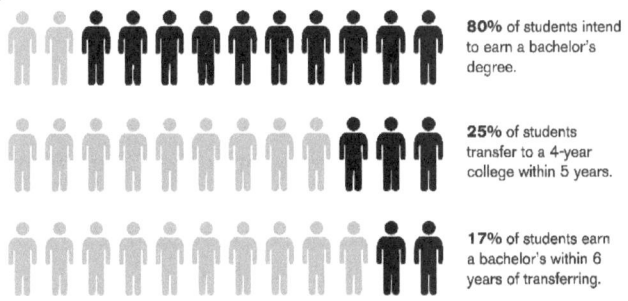

Source: https://ccrc.tc.columbia.edu/media/k2/attachments/what-we-know-about-transfer.pdf

Strategies for a Successful Vertical Transfer

Admission

One of the great features of transfer is that transfer students can postpone the admission decision as community colleges are open admission. Therefore, the admission decision can be delayed until the student starts the transfer process and seeks entry into the destination C/U.

The admission can be delayed for up to two years, and students can apply for admission when ready. All in all, a transfer student needs to be admitted by the destination C/U.

Colleges/universities (C/U) publish the admission requirements for transfer students on their websites and through the Common Data Set (CDS). Make sure you check both and take a close look at section D in the CDS. Here you'll find which semesters C/U accepts applications from transfer students. Plus, here, you'll discover how many students applied, were accepted, and enrolled. Depending on the C/U, you may find that the acceptance rate for transfer students may be lower than the acceptance rate for regular first-year applicants.

Additionally, section D includes information on whether the C/U requires transfer students to submit SAT/ACT scores as part of the admission application. Learning all this information now will help you plan and navigate the transfer process successfully. Remember, some C/U may choose not to complete or publish the CDS.

Students planning to follow the vertical transfer path should consider applying to more than one university because admission into the university of your choice is not always guaranteed. Therefore, it is wise to cast a wide net and be flexible. Remember Universal Truth #4 – *you have options*!

Credit Transfer

One of the main challenges associated with transfer is transferring credits.[119] In other words, it is not uncommon for college credits earned at various colleges to not transfer. Namely, students who complete credits at one institution – home institution – may not get recognition for these credits at another institution – destination institution. Hence students may need to repeat and pay for the same course(s) again. This can lead to increased college costs, delays in graduation, and lots of frustration.

Here are a few strategies on how to mitigate credit loss during transfer.

Colleges in Different States. It is pretty standard for students to want to transfer between institutions located in different states. However, credit transfer between these institutions tends to be quite challenging. Higher education professionals have been aware of this limitation, and they have been working to remedy it.

One step in this direction is the <u>Interstate Passport Initiative</u> set up by the Western Interstate Commission for Higher Education. This initiative allows seamless credit transfer for students attending colleges participating in this program.

If your teen plans to start at a community college in one state and then transfer to another C/U, you'll need to do a bit of research. First, visit the website for the destination C/U and look for the transfer admission section. Then, learn everything you can about the requirements of the destination institution. Plus, many C/U have dedicated transfer staff who can address your questions.

The sooner you learn about these requirements and contact the transfer admission officer at the destination C/U the smoother the transfer will be and the more credits your teen will manage to transfer.

Colleges in the Same State. Transferring credits between public community colleges and private C/U in the same state is possible. But the number of credit hours accepted for transfer by the private institution can vary significantly, as private C/U are not required to take them.

In essence, higher education institutions (community colleges, public and private colleges, and universities) function independently and have their own rules. This means they have full flexibility in deciding how to treat credits earned at other institutions. As you'll see later on, public community colleges and public universities tend to have state agreements that require transfer credits to be treated similarly within the same state. Private universities or liberal arts colleges are not usually covered by these agreements and hence have full flexibility in deciding how to treat transfer credits.

A student planning to start at a community college and transfer to a private C/U should contact the admission officer at the destination C/U and learn more about making the process as seamless as possible to retain as many credits as possible.

Public Colleges in the Same State. Transferring between public community colleges and public C/U in the same state is one of the best ways to capitalize on all the benefits of vertical transfer. Many states have established transfer agreements covering public community colleges, universities, and liberal arts colleges. To benefit from these agreements, students need to contact the admission officer at the destination C/U as soon as possible.

Completing a Credential Prior to Transferring. Completing a credential is something that can benefit students greatly when attempting to transfer credits between public colleges within the same state. The credential is the Associate of Arts (AA), typically a degree geared towards students who want to follow the vertical transfer path. One of the critical benefits of this degree is that the credits will be packaged under it, and the destination C/U will usually accept the full degree, as opposed to picking which credits to accept.

A study found that students who earned an AA before transfer were more likely to complete a bachelor's degree.[120]

Let's consider the following scenario for transferring between a public community college and a public C/U. Students A and B attended a community college and intended to transfer to complete a bachelor's degree. Student A completed the AA degree, but student B decided not to complete it.

As the transfer process involves an admission decision, both students must apply and get admitted to a C/U. Once accepted, student A is likely to transfer all the credits earned through the AA into the university because they completed the AA degree. Consequently, student A will likely start as a junior and may need to complete two more years of college to earn the bachelor's degree. Therefore, student A capitalizes on the savings associated with the vertical transfer process. This student pays lower tuition and fees for each credit hour completed at the public community college. Specifically, if the tuition per credit hour at the community college is $150 per credit and at the university $300 per credit, the total amount spent for tuition (fees excluded) for the bachelor's degree at the community college and university is 60 x $150 + 60 x $300 = $9,000 + $18,000 = $27,000.

Now let's consider student B. Student B started at the community college, took 55 credit hours, but did not complete an AA degree. Student B now decides to transfer to the public C/U to pursue a bachelor's degree. Because of a lack of a degree, when student B decides to transfer, the destination C/U can pick which credits it accepts during the transfer process. Because of that, student B has little control over the transfer process and may pay twice for some of the same courses. For the sake of argument, let's assume the university accepts 40 credits out of the 55 intended. Student B would enter the C/U as a sophomore and take 80 more credits to complete a bachelor's degree. Plus, it should be noted that losing more than 9 credit hours during the transfer process roughly equates to losing a semester's worth of course work. This leads to delays in graduation. The actual cost for the bachelor's degree for student B – assuming the same tuition rates as for student A – is 40 x $150 + 15 x $150 + 80 x $300 = $6,000 + $2,250 + $24,000 = $32,250 plus an extra semester delay in graduation.

Transfer Agreements with Admission Guarantees. The best way to capitalize on the benefits of vertical transfer is to use transfer agreements with transfer guarantees. The arrangements are usually established by two institutions, a community college, and a C/U. Under these agreements, students who meet specific criteria are guaranteed admission into the C/U.

These guaranteed agreements are set up as a separate transfer track at the community college. First, a student needs to meet specific criteria to get admitted into the track. Some of these criteria may include a certain HSGPA, high school course requirements in Math or English, and so on. Then the student is required to take a specific set of courses and maintain a college GPA above a certain threshold to be guaranteed transfer into the C/U. These tracks tend to be very prescriptive. Hence students may be required to take specific courses that count towards transfer starting with their first semester of freshman year.

One way to recognize these agreements is their name, and they tend to have the names of both colleges. The best way to find out about these agreements is to go to the community college or the C/U websites.

***

Remember, there are nuances to college transfer. Depending on the C/U, the decision for credit transfer lies with different offices. In some instances, the decision for credit transfer is centralized – one office reviews and accepts credits. In other cases, various departments review and accept credits.

All in all, states and colleges have their own rules governing transfer. However, the strategies presented in this chapter can ensure a smooth transfer process, help students graduate on time, and keep college expenses to a minimum.

Please get familiar with the transfer requirements for the destination college. That will ensure that your teen enrolls and completes only the courses they need to at the initial college before transferring to the new one.

Remember, many C/U have specialized staff within their Admissions Offices focused on transfer. Get in touch with them and learn as much information as possible about the transfer requirements at the destination C/U. This will ensure that your teen completes all the right courses, understands the college GPA requirements, and starts the process when needed. The sooner you do it, the smoother the transfer process.

This section aims to help parents and students take advantage of all the benefits of vertical transfer and discuss strategies that will ensure a smooth transfer. Community colleges have been making a massive difference in students' lives by providing access to an excellent education, resources, and, most importantly, great economic mobility. Community colleges are great economic drivers in our communities, and many successful professionals started their college careers at a community college. Therefore, the benefits and the value provided by community colleges are massive. Use the strategies discussed in this chapter to make sure that you can capitalize on the low tuition opportunities.

***

Summary

We are almost there. This part of the book provided information on keeping college costs low and helping your teen graduate with a bachelor's degree as soon as possible.

If you make it a point to go through this part before committing to a college, you'll benefit from it and will be able to save money on college. Because knowing if a college uses a decrease or replace policy when awarding credit for high school courses can help you save thousands of dollars on tuition and fees.

Then, knowing how to guide your teen in college can help you save some more. The reality is that we all get excited about new things and stages of life, and college is no exception. All this excitement can drive first-year students to take on a heavy course load for the freshman year and then start working to bring in some personal expense money. Keeping in mind the freshman year transition, the course load, and how these can lead to burn-out, frustration, and decreases in GPA can also help you save money on college.

Finally, understanding the nuances of transfer can help you decide now about the best path forward for your teen. For example, suppose the community college is the best way for you and your teen to go forward. In that case, you now have strategies and information on navigating the transfer process, and lowering your college costs.

Conclusion

Phew – you are almost done! You've been through a roller coaster of stress, anxiety, endless to-do lists, and activities, but the prize is in sight. This is the time to take a step back and look at all the work you and your teen did. A huge milestone – high school graduation – is right around the corner. Then a life-changing moment is approaching fast – leaving for college. After that, nothing will be the same again. Know that all the hard work and due diligence you and your teen put in every day, every week, and every year has paid off.

Now you know everything about smart college selection and how to find and use college statistics to help you identify the colleges with the best academic, personal, and financial fit. You have learned all there is to know about college application plans and how to select the ones that would be most beneficial to you and your teen. Then we discussed the materials you'd need for the college application and how to go about filing the financial aid applications. College decisions were next. Here we focused on understanding the different decisions, why colleges use them, and how to navigate them to identify the college that your teen should commit to by May 1st. Finally, we discussed various strategies on how to keep college costs low. This last part could help you with the college decision, as this information could help you save lots of money on college.

None of this was easy, but you've made it. This is the time to celebrate, thank everyone who helped you along the way, enjoy friendships, and make lifelong memories.

This is the best time to consider reading the second book in this series – The Ultimate College Financial Aid Guide: Understand the Aid Offer & Ask For More Money. It will help you ascertain the last component of college fit, namely the financial fit. This book will help you make sense of the offer of financial assistance, compare colleges on costs, and help you ask for more aid. For more details scan the QR code below:

Now is the time for your teen to spread their wings and soar as they prepare for their future. You did your absolute best, and I am sure they will make you proud as they pursue their dreams and make our world a better place.

Congratulations! You and your teen did it!

Before you go, I want to ask for a tiny favor. If you got anything out of this book, had any sort of "aha" moment, or felt that the information provided here made a difference for you or your teen, please consider giving a copy of it to someone else, leaving a review, making a video, commenting about it on social media, or anything, really – anything to show that you found it beneficial and that it may help others navigate the college admissions maze successfully. It would mean a lot to me.

List of Key Terms

- C/U or C/Us – Liberal Arts College(s) or University(ies)
- SAI/EFC – the Student Aid Index (SAI) replaces the Expected Family Contribution (EFC) effective October 1, 2022. The SAI is "an index that reflects an evaluation of a student's approximate financial resources to contribute toward the student's postsecondary education for the academic year."
- Gift aid - money that does not have to be repaid, i.e., scholarships, grants, waivers, etc.
- Scholarships – merit aid, awarded typically because of academic achievement
- Grants – need based aid, awarded typically because of demonstrated financial need
- Institutional aid – funds sourced from the college/university budget

- NPC – Net Price Calculator
- FAFSA – Free Application for Federal Student Aid
- CSS Profile - College Scholarship Service Profile
- COA – cost of attendance
- Net Price or Out-of-Pocket Costs (OPC) –cost of attendance minus gift aid
- Applied – students who submitted applications
- Admitted – students who were admitted
- Enrolled – students who enrolled, from the ones that were admitted
- Open admission – every students who applies is admitted
- Selectivity rate – percent of students who were admitted out of the ones that applied
- Yield rate – percent of students who enrolled out of the ones that were admitted

References

Geiser, S., & Santelices, M. V. (2007). Validity of High-School Grades in Predicting Student Success beyond the Freshman Year: High-School Record vs. Standardized Tests as Indicators of Four-Year College Outcomes. Research & Occasional Paper Series: CSHE. 6.07. *Center for studies in higher education*.

Hayes, S. K. (2010). Student employment and the economic cost of delayed college graduation. *Journal of Business & Leadership: Research, Practice, and Teaching (2005-2012)*, 6(1), 129-140.

Jenkins, D., & Fink, J. (2015). What we know about transfer. New York, NY: Columbia University, Teachers College, Community College Research Center.

Simone, S.A. (2014). Transferability of Postsecondary Credit Following Student Transfer or Coenrollment

(NCES 2014-163). U.S. Department of Education. Washington, DC: National Center for Education Statistics. Retrieved [date] from http://nces.ed.gov/pubsearch.

Acknowledgements

It takes a village to write a book and this one is no exception.

I am especially grateful to my husband Adrian for all his support and encouragements during this time. His kind nudges and encouragements helped me put one foot in front of another when the research, writing, and publishing process became overwhelming. He was there to discuss with me each section of the book, its flow, and logic.

Much appreciation for and gratefulness for three Ladies in my life. I am extremely grateful to my dear mentor Dr. Gita Pitter for our extensive conversations on complex concepts and college and university expectations. Grateful for our walks and extremely informative conversations on issues that parents and students face regarding college selection, admission, and finances.
A heartfelt thank you to my dear friend Dr. Maya Ackerman for her unconditional friendship and support

over the years. For reading and providing feedback on the book and graciously agreeing to write the foreword to it. I am deeply grateful for our friendship and collaboration.

My sincere thanks to my dear friend Dr. Lauren Haddad-Freidman for all her support throughout this process. Her reading, editing, and questioning have helped polish this book.

A sincere thank you to everyone who read and provided feedback for the book that helped polish it – Alan Lupsha and Laurie Knitter. Also, many thanks to Kim Crone and Otis Miller, III, for graciously addressing my questions.

About the Author

Diana Barbu, Ph.D., is committed to helping students graduate in four years with the least amount of debt. Dr. Diana served as the Associate Vice-Provost of Institutional Research and Effectiveness at St. Thomas University, as the Director of Research and Data Analytics at Miami Dade College, and as the Director of Academic Programs at The State University System of Florida – Board of Governors. She holds a Ph.D. in Higher Education from Florida State University, a Master in Communication from Rutgers University, and a Bachelor of Science in Computer Science and Mathematics.

Using her senior leadership experience at public and private colleges, Dr. Diana points parents and students to accurate, actionable information to help with the college admission decision. She offers strategies and tools to help parents and students find the best academic and financial fit for their unique needs.

Notes

[1] https://www.insidehighered.com/news/survey/2020-survey-admissions-leaders

[2] https://www.insidehighered.com/news/survey/2020-survey-admissions-leaders

[3] https://www.insidehighered.com/admissions/article/2019/12/16/justice-department-sues-and-settles-college-admissions-group

[4] https://www.nacacnet.org/globalassets/documents/publications/research/2018_soca/soca2019_all.pdf

[5] https://www.fairtest.org/1700-colleges-and-universities-do-not-require-SAT-for-2022%20and%20https:/fairtest.org/

[6] https://sites.gatech.edu/admission-blog/

[7] https://www.nacacfairs.org/learn/search/college-types/

[8] https://www.nacacnet.org/globalassets/documents/publications/research/2018_soca/soca2019_all.pdf

[9] https://www.nacacnet.org/globalassets/documents/publications/research/2018_soca/soca2019_all.pdf

[10] https://www.nacacnet.org/globalassets/documents/publications/research/2018_soca/soca2019_all.pdf

[11] https://www.nacacnet.org/globalassets/documents/publications/research/2018_soca/soca2019_all.pdf

[12] https://www.nacacnet.org/globalassets/documents/publications/research/2018_soca/soca2019_all.pdf

[13] https://www.princetonreview.com/college-rankings/college-hopes-worries

[14] https://nces.ed.gov/pubs2018/2018434.pdf

[15] https://journals.psu.edu/mentor/article/view/61278/60911

[16] https://journals.psu.edu/mentor/article/view/61278/60911

[17] https://www.nacacnet.org/news--publications/Research/character-and-the-college-admission-process/

[18] https://cshe.berkeley.edu/sites/default/files/publications/rops.geiser._sat_6.13.07.pdf

[19] https://commondataset.org/wp-content/uploads/2020/04/CDS_2019-2020.pdf

[20] https://www.washingtonpost.com/news/grade-point/wp/2017/10/13/the-science-behind-selective-colleges/

[21] https://www.washingtonpost.com/news/grade-point/wp/2017/10/13/the-science-behind-selective-colleges/

[22] https://www.washingtonpost.com/news/grade-point/wp/2017/10/13/the-science-behind-selective-colleges/

[23] https://www.insidehighered.com/quicktakes/2021/05/17/no-more-sat-or-act-u-california

[24] https://www.fairtest.org/1700-colleges-and-universities-do-not-require-SAT-for-2022

[25] https://www.insidehighered.com/news/survey/2021-survey-admissions-leaders-finds-32-had-filled-classes-may-1

[26] https://www.fidelity.com/bin-public/060_www_fidelity_com/documents/about-fidelity/fidelity-college-savings-student-debt-study-fact-sheet.pdf

[27] https://www.brookings.edu/research/time-to-graduation-too-often-overlooked/

[28] https://nces.ed.gov/programs/digest/d20/tables/dt20_326.10.asp?referer=raceindica.asp

[29] https://nces.ed.gov/fastfacts/display.asp?id=40

[30] https://www.nacacnet.org/globalassets/documents/publications/research/2018_soca/soca2019_all.pdf

31 https://www.researchgate.net/profile/Ray-Franke/publication/249644731_Completing_College_Assessing_Graduation_Rates_at_Four-Year_Institutions/links/0046351e5bb5279e3a000000/Completing-College-Assessing-Graduation-Rates-at-Four-Year-Institutions.pdf

32 https://www.washingtonpost.com/news/grade-point/wp/2017/10/13/the-science-behind-selective-colleges/

33 https://ed.stanford.edu/sites/default/files/challenge_success_white_paper_on_college_admissions_10.1.2018-reduced.pdf

34 https://ed.stanford.edu/sites/default/files/challenge_success_white_paper_on_college_admissions_10.1.2018-reduced.pdf

35 https://www.insidehighered.com/admissions/article/2018/10/15/stanford-study-says-rankings-do-not-point-students-best-college-fit

36 https://www.insidehighered.com/admissions/article/2018/10/15/stanford-study-says-rankings-do-not-point-students-best-college-fit

37 https://ed.stanford.edu/sites/default/files/challenge_success_white_paper_on_college_admissions_10.1.2018-reduced.pdf

38 https://ed.stanford.edu/sites/default/files/challenge_success_white_paper_on_college_admissions_10.1.2018-reduced.pdf

39

https://ed.stanford.edu/sites/default/files/challenge_success_white_paper_on_college_admissions_10.1.2018-reduced.pdf

40

https://ed.stanford.edu/sites/default/files/challenge_success_white_paper_on_college_admissions_10.1.2018-reduced.pdf

41

https://ed.stanford.edu/sites/default/files/challenge_success_white_paper_on_college_admissions_10.1.2018-reduced.pdf

42 https://www.usnews.com/education/best-colleges/articles/common-app

43 https://www.latimes.com/opinion/story/2022-02-21/editorial-whats-less-fair-than-the-sat-you-might-be-surprised

44 https://www.princetonreview.com/college-advice/early-action-vs-early-decision#:~:text=You%20may%20not%20apply%20to,to%20apply%20to%20other%20schools.

45

https://www.nacacnet.org/globalassets/documents/publications/DefinitionsofAdmissionOptionsinHigherEducation.pdf

46

https://www.insidehighered.com/admissions/views/2020/02/24/early-decision-calculations-are-different-nacac-changed-its-rules

47 https://www.princetonreview.com/college-advice/early-action-vs-early-decision#:~:text=You%20may%20not%20apply%20to,to%20apply%20to%20other%20schools

48

https://www.nacacnet.org/globalassets/documents/publications/DefinitionsofAdmissionOptionsinHigherEducation.pdf

49

https://www.nacacnet.org/globalassets/documents/publications/research/2018_soca/soca2019_all.pdf

50

https://www.nacacnet.org/globalassets/documents/publications/research/2018_soca/soca2019_all.pdf

51 https://www.usnews.com/education/best-colleges/paying-for-college/articles/2018-10-03/how-applying-early-for-college-affects-financial-aid

52

https://www.insidehighered.com/admissions/views/2020/02/24/early-decision-calculations-are-different-nacac-changed-its-rules

53 https://www.usnews.com/education/best-colleges/paying-for-college/articles/2018-10-03/how-applying-early-for-college-affects-financial-aid

54

https://www.insidehighered.com/admissions/views/2020/02/24/early-decision-calculations-are-different-nacac-changed-its-rules

55

https://www.nacacnet.org/globalassets/documents/publications/research/2018_soca/soca2019_all.pdf

56 https://www.usnews.com/education/best-colleges/articles/2017-12-04/everything-you-need-to-know-about-college-instant-decision-days

57 https://www.insidehighered.com/news/survey/2021-survey-admissions-leaders-finds-32-had-filled-classes-may-1

58 https://www.washingtonpost.com/news/grade-point/wp/2017/10/13/the-science-behind-selective-colleges/

59 https://www.usnews.com/education/best-colleges/articles/common-app

60 https://www.coalitionforcollegeaccess.org/mycoalition-counselor-all/when-does-the-coalition-application-open

61 https://apstudents.collegeboard.org/sending-scores/free-score-send

62 https://www.usnews.com/education/best-colleges/articles/common-app

63 https://www2.ed.gov/about/reports/annual/2019report/fsa-report.pdf

64 https://studentaid.gov/complete-aid-process/how-calculated

65 https://masfaa.org/wp-content/uploads/2021/06/Consolidated-Appropriations-Act-2021.pdf

66 https://www.forbes.com/advisor/student-loans/fafsa-changes/

67 https://studentaid.gov/understand-aid/eligibility

[68] https://studentaid.gov/understand-aid/eligibility

[69] https://studentaid.gov/apply-for-aid/fafsa/filling-out/dependency

[70] https://studentaid.gov/apply-for-aid/fafsa/filling-out/dependency

[71] https://finaid.org/educators/pj/dependencyoverrides/

[72] https://studentaid.gov/apply-for-aid/fafsa/filling-out

[73] https://www.youtube.com/watch?v=1c1gNefSw78&feature=youtu.be&ab_channel=FederalStudentAid

[74] https://studentaid.gov/help/how-long

[75] https://studentaid.gov/help/fsa-id

[76] https://studentaid.gov/help/fsa-id

[77] https://studentaid.gov/apply-for-aid/fafsa/filling-out/dependency

[78] https://www.usnews.com/education/best-colleges/paying-for-college/articles/2015/03/02/do-4-things-if-your-fafsa-is-selected-for-verification

[79] https://studentaid.gov/understand-aid/types/work-study

[80] https://studentaid.gov/understand-aid/types/work-study

[81] https://www.youtube.com/watch?v=1c1gNefSw78&feature=youtu.be&ab_channel=FederalStudentAid

82 https://studentaid.gov/apply-for-aid/fafsa/review-and-correct/review

83 https://studentaid.gov/apply-for-aid/fafsa/review-and-correct/review

84 https://studentaid.gov/apply-for-aid/fafsa/review-and-correct/review

85 https://www.youtube.com/watch?v=1c1gNefSw78&feature=youtu.be&ab_channel=FederalStudentAid

86 https://www.usnews.com/education/best-colleges/paying-for-college/articles/2017-08-02/how-expected-family-contribution-for-college-is-calculated

87 https://cssprofile.collegeboard.org/getting-started-your-css-profile-application

88 https://www.floridastudentfinancialaidsg.org/SAPHome/SAPHome?url=home

89 https://studentaid.gov/help/info-needed

90 https://www.insidehighered.com/print/admissions/article/2021/03/29/many-expect-waiting-lists-be-worse-ever-year

91 https://sites.gatech.edu/admission-blog/

92 https://www.nacacnet.org/globalassets/documents/publications/research/2018_soca/soca2019_all.pdf

93 https://www.insidehighered.com/print/admissions/article/2021/03/29/many-expect-waiting-lists-be-worse-ever-year.

94 https://www.insidehighered.com/print/admissions/article/2021/03/29/many-expect-waiting-lists-be-worse-ever-year.

95 https://www.insidehighered.com/print/admissions/article/2021/03/29/many-expect-waiting-lists-be-worse-ever-year.

96 https://sites.gatech.edu/admission-blog/

97 https://www.insidehighered.com/print/admissions/article/2021/03/29/many-expect-waiting-lists-be-worse-ever-year.

98 https://www.insidehighered.com/print/admissions/article/2021/03/29/many-expect-waiting-lists-be-worse-ever-year.

99 https://www.nacacnet.org/globalassets/documents/publications/research/2018_soca/soca2019_all.pdf

100 https://www.insidehighered.com/print/admissions/article/2021/03/29/many-expect-waiting-lists-be-worse-ever-year.

101 https://www.insidehighered.com/admissions/article/2018/04/02/colleges-and-high-schools-again-debate-use-waiting-lists-admissions

102 https://www.insidehighered.com/print/admissions/article/2021/03/29/many-expect-waiting-lists-be-worse-ever-year.

[103] https://sites.gatech.edu/admission-blog/2021/03/23/the-waitlist-why/

[104] https://sites.gatech.edu/admission-blog

[105] https://sites.gatech.edu/admission-blog/

[106] https://sites.gatech.edu/admission-blog/

[107] https://www.petersons.com/blog/what-the-waitlist-or-a-deferral-means-for-your-college-acceptance/

[108] https://sites.gatech.edu/admission-blog/

[109] https://www.petersons.com/blog/what-the-waitlist-or-a-deferral-means-for-your-college-acceptance/

[110] https://www.petersons.com/blog/what-the-waitlist-or-a-deferral-means-for-your-college-acceptance/

[111] https://sites.gatech.edu/admission-blog/

[112] https://sites.gatech.edu/admission-blog/

[113] https://sites.gatech.edu/admission-blog/

[114] https://www.petersons.com/blog/what-the-waitlist-or-a-deferral-means-for-your-college-acceptance/

[115] https://www.insidehighered.com/quicktakes/2019/03/12/more-confusion-credit-hour-definition#:~:text=According%20to%20federal%20rules%20established,qualifies%20for%20federal%20financial%20aid.

[116] https://scholars.fhsu.edu/cgi/viewcontent.cgi?article=1163&

context=jbl#:~:text=The%20expected%20economic%20cost%20of,year%20is%20estimated%20at%20%2494%2C921.

117

https://ccrc.tc.columbia.edu/media/k2/attachments/what-we-know-about-transfer.pdf

118

https://ccrc.tc.columbia.edu/media/k2/attachments/what-we-know-about-transfer.pdf

119

https://ccrc.tc.columbia.edu/media/k2/attachments/what-we-know-about-transfer.pdf

120

https://ccrc.tc.columbia.edu/media/k2/attachments/what-we-know-about-transfer.pdf

Made in United States
Troutdale, OR
04/24/2024

19340626R00148